The Rooftop Busker

NEW WRITING SCOTLAND 33

Edited by
Gerry Cambridge
and
Diana Hendry

Gaelic adviser:
Rody Gorman

D1350857

Association for Scottish Literary Studies

Association for Scottish Literary Studies
Scottish Literature, 7 University Gardens
University of Glasgow, Glasgow G12 8QH
www.asls.org.uk

ASLS is a registered charity no. SC006535

First published 2015

British Library Cataloguing in Publication Data

A CIP record for this book is available
from the British Library

ISBN 978-1-906841-24-9

W. G. Sebald quotations on pp. 60 and 64 are from
Sebald, W. G., *A Place in the Country*, translated by Jo Catling
(London: Hamish Hamilton, 2013)

The Association for Scottish Literary Studies
acknowledges the support of Creative Scotland
towards the publication of this book

ALBA | CHRUTHACHAIL

Printed by Bell & Bain Ltd, Glasgow

CONTENTS

INTRODUCTION

This number of *New Writing Scotland* marks the departure of Zoë Strachan as co-editor and the arrival of Diana Hendry. As well as being a poet in her own right, Diana is also a widely published fiction writer both for young people and adults, and this helps address the (potential) imbalance of two poets deciding on submissions of fiction.

Co-editing is an interesting process. It helps if there is some sense of centrality of judgement or aesthetic shared by the two editors, with perhaps some uncommon ground on either side to allow for the unexpected and perhaps even a bit of bartering before one ends up at an edited volume that both editors can be happy with.

Yet, where *New Writing Scotland* is concerned, 'editing' is perhaps a problematic term. *New Writing Scotland* is not edited, for instance, in the way that my magazine *The Dark Horse* is edited – where I am often interventionist and hands-on, especially with the prose, putting each piece through numerous copy-edits. Rather, the work published in *New Writing Scotland* is *selected*; there is neither time nor space for the editorial input I would make with the *Horse*. One effect of this is that the work as it is sent in to *New Writing Scotland* has to be wholly finished and polished *as it is submitted*. There is neither space nor time for editors to get back to a particular author requesting, say, more work on an ending, a beginning, or a considered-problematic stylistic element. With *New Writing Scotland*, we deal only in the absolutes of *yes* and *no*.

Editing – selecting – can also hold a mirror up to the self as editor. Diana was, I think, surprised by the number of writers submitting who were known to her personally, in some cases well-known. Twenty years of editing *The Dark Horse* have steeled me in such matters to regarding uncomfortable decisions as a wholly professional business, and to relying on writing friends and acquaintances regarding the process in like manner. But these are not easy issues, particularly in a concentrated, at times carnaptious, Scottish literary scene. As I know from long experience, it helps in the selection process – insofar as one is able – to think of the reading, as opposed to the writing, community. A showcase such as *New Writing Scotland* is not a showcase for the creative writing industry as administered in the universities – though some of its contents may well come from there. It is, though, a showcase for the 'best' writing submitted – at least by the estimates of the two editors – wherever that may originate from. There was some early debate when selecting work as to whether submissions should again be considered anonymously. Generally speaking, I felt not, but Diana may wish to bring that in, with her new co-editor's agreement, in her own final year as co-editor, which will be 2017.

Lastly, the submission deadline for this year's anthology was considerably extended to make allowance for any responses to the Scottish Referendum of 18 September, 2014, to filter in. As it happened, very few of the submissions dealing with this, or the new political atmosphere in the country, seemed of much value. They varied from the obvious to the rollickingly one-dimensional (which can both have their place, given sufficient verbal force), but there was a distinct lack of obliqueness, subtlety, or that refusal 'to falsify the ambiguities' that Robert Frost mentioned in another context. It remains to be seen how the new political dispensation in Scotland will make itself felt in Scottish writing – which may be apparent in *New Writing Scotland* 34 next year.

Gerry Cambridge

NEW WRITING SCOTLAND 34: SUBMISSION INSTRUCTIONS

The thirty-fourth volume of *New Writing Scotland* will be published in summer 2016. Submissions are invited from writers resident in Scotland or Scots by birth, upbringing or inclination. All forms of writing are welcome: autobiography and memoirs; creative responses to events and experiences; drama; graphic artwork (monochrome only); poetry; political and cultural commentary and satire; short fiction; travel writing or any other creative prose may be submitted, but not full-length plays or novels, though self-contained extracts are acceptable. The work must not be previously published, submitted, or accepted for publication elsewhere, and may be in any of the languages of Scotland.

Submissions should be typed on one side of the paper only and the sheets secured at the top left corner. Prose pieces should be double-spaced and carry an approximate word-count. **You should provide a covering letter, clearly marked with your name and address. *Please also put your name on the individual works*.** If you would like to receive an acknowledgement of receipt of your manuscript, please enclose a stamped addressed postcard. If you would like to be informed if your submission is unsuccessful, or would like your submissions returned, you should enclose a stamped addressed envelope with sufficient postage. Submissions should be sent by **30 September 2015**, in an A4 envelope, to the address below. We are sorry but we cannot accept submissions by fax or email.

Please be aware that we have limited space in each edition, and therefore shorter pieces are more suitable – although longer items of exceptional quality may still be included. **Please send no more than four poems, or one prose work**. Successful contributors will be paid at the rate of £20 per published page. Authors retain all rights to their work(s), and are free to submit and/or publish the same work(s) elsewhere after they appear in *New Writing Scotland*.

ASLS
Scottish Literature
7 University Gardens
University of Glasgow
Glasgow G12 8QH, Scotland

Tel +44 (0)141 330 5309
www.asls.org.uk

Juana Adcock

HOW REPTILES GROW THEIR TAILS BACK

'I don't have time to look after you,' I said, but didn't look away.

Even after the accident, I was bewitched by Raf's beautiful green scales, his timid crest, his cold abdomen, his tiny claws. His tail coiling around my arm. His toothless, sharp mouth, good for chomping vegetables.

He has only ever bitten me once, but that was my own fault: I spent too long on the phone, knowing how much he hates it. Whenever he hears a phone ring, he whips his tail against the glass walls of his terrarium, maddened pupils dilating and contracting. I don't like to upset him, but that day I needed to sort out some issues with the bank. After I hung up I took Raf out of his terrarium. He pretended to be tame, but as soon as I was off guard he clung to my finger. The harder I tried to pull him away, the stronger he tightened his jaw. I bled a little; the scar can barely be seen now.

This was before the accident, though. Now he wasn't quite as spirited. I would hold him softly between my thumb and index finger, as if a very fragile egg. His head, limbs and tail hung languidly. He was paler. Transparent, almost.

I still had a few minutes before I had to leave for work. I switched on the lamp, and spread him belly-up on the table, pinning his limbs flat with my fingers. The skin had deep, decrepit furrows around his joints. His tail was growing back, just. The scratches were black against the green scales and the wound around his left eye was moist and sullen. I pushed his chin up with my little finger, stretching the neck membranes. The scales' pattern on his rib cage seemed very human and yet completely alien. Or was it more like an alocasia leaf? Through his skin I could see his purplish organs. I closed one eye, then opened it and closed the other. My vision was blurred in the right eye. It wasn't the first time I'd noticed. I need to go to the optometrist, I thought. Maybe on a Saturday.

'I'm late for work. I'll feed you as soon as I get back, okay?' I said, trying to sound as casual as possible. I hadn't prepared Raf's food that morning. Alfalfa, coriander, courgette, a whiz of the blender and a

crushed multi-vitamin tablet mixed in. I'd done a lot of research, and
nobody seemed to be quite clear on whether or not adding human
multi-vitamins would help, but I had to do something. I used a plastic
spoon to force the mush down Raf's throat. He refused to eat on his
own since the accident, didn't like me feeding him either, and would
often spit everything back out. It wasn't a very pleasant job for the
mornings, but it had to be done before going to work because my
evenings were too irregular – working overtime, business dinners and
seeing Alex as well. Recovery requires stability, regularity.

   Or such was my theory. But after fourteen weeks of following this
regime and not seeing any results, I was starting to doubt whether it
made any difference. Once or twice I tried to tell him that his attitude
affected his health as well. 'Whatever I do will not help if you don't
make an effort,' I explained. 'I need you to try, at least a little bit, okay?'
But he wouldn't budge. I kept feeding him anyway. I didn't want him
to die.

Alex worked in the same building as me but in another department.
He looked like the model from a perfume ad that was showing on TV
at the time. The girls in the office were so jealous. My assistant said,
'You seem to be on a roll.' And it was true. For some reason I'd been
doing exceptionally well. A big promotion, a bigger office with a nice
view, a pay raise sufficient to start paying off my debts. But most of all
I felt good, from the inside out. I liked walking down the street, glancing
at my reflection in storefront windows. Nicely cut overcoat, sleek slacks
and five-hundred-dollar heels; leather gloves, a designer haircut, those
sunglasses I bought in Tokyo … With so many good things happening
it was only natural to not want to spend all my time with a terminally
ill reptile. It was such a hassle, for example, when I spent the night at
Alex's on a weekday, because I had to get up earlier to go home and
feed Raf before work, instead of showing up at work together, in the
same car, as I know Alex would have wanted. I never told Alex I had
Raf to look after. I made excuses, saying I liked to get ready in the
morning in my own house, with my own things. He did complain, once,
along the lines of 'If you don't keep any of your things at my place, and
don't invite me to your place either, it means you're afraid of commit-
ment.' I hurled back that we didn't need to keep seeing each other in

that case. He never so much as peeped again. At least not until after the wedding.

When I got back home from work that night I didn't feed Raf straight away as I had promised. In fact, I didn't even look in his direction. I went straight past him into my bedroom, got into some comfy clothes, and padded into the kitchen to switch on the TV and put dinner in the oven.

While I chewed my bland meal staring at the ads, I understood that he would never eat again, or even move voluntarily. He was barely more than a faded vegetable that would probably never recover. Watering him from time to time should be sufficient, I thought.

But on my way to bed I caught sight of something odd about him. I came closer, and saw a black, thick scab had formed on the wound in his left eye. I went back into the kitchen, made his mush and fed him, saying, 'This is the last time I do this, okay?' We both knew I didn't really mean that, but I didn't know what else to say. How did I get into this? It was not right.

I'm still not sure how the accident happened. I came in one night and found the terrarium shattered on the floor, soil and broken glass everywhere, Raf nowhere to be seen. It must have been a cat. I found him lying half-dead on my pillow, tail chewed off. I tried not to feel guilty about it, but I did. I should have closed the window, I should have kept the terrarium in a safer place, I should have given him more loving attention.

I went to bed, and woke up at five a.m. from a nightmare. Shattered, I took my pillow to the living room and switched on the TV. It was the first of July, 2007. I know the exact date because it was the tenth anniversary of the day Britain divested its power over Hong Kong. I watched how sad everyone was, the heroic speech in the rain, the band playing the hymn, the British flag being lowered. Men in suits walked with their heads downcast, and repeated: *this is not a day of sadness, but of rejoicing.* The old empire gave up yet another of its territories and China recovered its command. China, which would soon extend its dominion over the earth. The last British governor of Hong Kong looked almost as sad as my Raf. I wondered if he, too, needed to be fed when he got

home. And I suddenly hated myself for my magnanimity. Who was I
to feed Raf, or anyone?

I thought of my breasts, my capacity to produce milk like a cow and
feed a living creature. What a degrading glandular system, what a
disgusting reproductive apparatus; like cattle we are, we mammals.

But Raf is not a mammal. I have no place feeding him. I shall never
do it again, I said to myself.

Time swept by. I came and went, and fasting Raf sat quietly in his
terrarium on the little table in the hall, illuminated by a sun-ray simu-
lating lamp. The temperature and humidity regulator were in good
working order. I passed by him on the way from the bathroom to my
bedroom, from my bedroom to the kitchen, from the kitchen to the
cupboard in the hall. He ignored me. His water basin slowly dried up.
Mould covered his plate, unwashed since the last time I fed him. The
peat moss clogged with faeces.

'If you don't make an effort, I won't either, okay?' I told him again
and again, but he wouldn't listen. 'At least change position, and I'll fill
your water basin,' but he still wouldn't move.

Sometimes I managed to not think about it, to pass through the hall
as if it were empty – without a terrarium standing there, interfering;
all I had to do was conform to the order of the days. But there were
one or two occasions on which his indifference drove me mad, and I
seized him in a frenzy, shaking him and yelling, 'Snap out of it! Move,
you despicable piece of thing! Do you not care? Is this how you repay
me for all the time I've spent taking care of you?!'

Once, in the middle of one of these fits, I remembered what Laszlo
used to say to me, when we were still at university. 'How can you be
so cold, so cruel? I don't get so much as a blink of sympathy for my
feelings!'

I would never reply, but just close my bedroom door. Laszlo would
knock, and show me a large bar of tablet broken into pieces. I would wil-
lingly take some. And then he would say, 'I'll leave it on the kitchen
table, just in case you want some more.' He knew me well, the beast. I
would tiptoe into the kitchen in the middle of the night trying to get
some more without being seen, but Laszlo, always on the lookout, would
intercept me. I knew, our friends had told me, that he did not really

care for me, that he could never truly love me unless we got married. Laszlo didn't want a girlfriend, a lover, or a flatmate, but a wife.

'And he wants a good, durable wife, one who can produce at least five children,' they'd say. 'And he has the money to keep them, and for her to be comfortable. He's a good man, he'd take good care of her.' But I couldn't care less about Laszlo.

While shaking Raf, I thought about Laszlo holding me gently between his giant fingers, extracting me from my terrarium, that is to say my bedroom, my limbs hanging languidly. I remembered the indifference with which I let Laszlo lay me down under the lamp to study my body, blue and green veins showing under my skin. I remembered his eyes closing at ejaculation, and his cardiac muscle beating against my chest. How he would fall asleep, exhausted like a child in its mother's arms. Except I was not his mother, and did not embrace him, or indeed move at all.

It became more and more nauseating to have Raf around. His terrarium smelled, but I didn't want to clean it. Even wearing rubber gloves, I couldn't bear touching him. I continued to have nightmares. I was tormented by his pupils, his tail that should be long and beautiful but was just a stump. I dreamed of a giant Raf that would swallow me to make me live in his intestines, or nail me to the ground with his claws, paralysing me.

I thought I might feel better if I hid the terrarium somewhere, so I wouldn't have to see him every time I went from one room to another. This way I could also bring Alex home without having to explain about Raf. I covered the terrarium with a thick cloth and put it in the back room. I locked the door; absurdly I felt safer this way.

Two months went by, during which I hardly visited him. I tried to focus on enjoying my perfect life. I bought a new car, and on a weekend break in the mountains Alex proposed to me, making me again the envy of all my female colleagues. Raf, safely locked in his room, could not interfere.

The first of September of that same year I was watching a special on Princess Diana's death on TV when I realised the vision in my right eye was very poor. I closed my left eye, then closed the right one. And again. The difference was significant, even though the optometrist had recently diagnosed me with perfect twenty-twenty vision. I had the deranged certainty that Raf's apathy was starting to grow like a cataract in my right eye. I was even afraid I might get a black scab like his. I went to his room and pulled off the cloth that covered the terrarium. There he was, breathing slightly. The scab was still as big, but for some reason Raf didn't seem abominable any more. He was just a beautifully sad, lonely creature. I was filled with compassion. I reached for the water mister, and sprayed water on his head; he soaked up some of the droplets with his tongue. For the first time since the accident, Raf actually looked at me with his healthy eye. I smiled at him, feeling much better, and covered the terrarium again. That night Alex and I made love desperately, as if the world was about to end.

*

A couple of years into our marriage, I wanted to celebrate. I got in the car with a bottle of champagne and a new state-of-the-art humidity regulator, and went to see Raf, who now lived in a luxury terrarium, locked in an industrial unit I rented in the suburbs, to keep Alex from finding him.

When I stepped under the metal curtain and switched on the neon strip lights on the ceiling, I was stunned by something bright green shooting up one of the plastic branches in the terrarium. Raf's limbs were strong, his eyes were sharp and focused, and the scab had disappeared. I, on the other hand, still had blurred vision in my right eye, despite the hypnotherapy, acupuncture and homeopathic treatments I'd undertaken, having exhausted all the avenues of Western medicine.

Unthinkingly, I drove to the nearest supermarket to buy some courgettes. I hadn't fed Raf for such a long time; now it just seemed like the thing to do. As Raf chomped away, I remembered the delight I used to take in his appetite, long ago. I gave him water, which he lapped up avidly. He whipped his tail, which had grown a great deal since the last time I went to see him, as if preparing for a duel. It was a miraculous change. His skin was even brighter than before the accident, with more shades of green and more beautiful patterns created by the smooth alignment of the scales. For a moment I resisted. I wanted him to be half-dead, lethargic as he was before. But his eyes, his maddened pupils, subjugated me.

*

What happened over the next few weeks was as predictable as it was inevitable. The company I worked for went bankrupt, and Alex and I both lost our jobs. Inflation skyrocketed and the stock market suffered the worst crash in recorded history. All my investments shrank to crumbs. But I couldn't care less. I started visiting Raf more regularly, to feed him, and spent the rest of my time just sitting there on the couch watching the news, refusing to get worried about any of it. Closing one eye and then the other, trying to figure out if my vision was still blurry. Alex, wild with jealousy, would pick a fight over any little thing, throw plates against the wall, make all sorts of threats in trying to get me to confess I had a lover, or that I didn't love him. But I wouldn't budge.

Then one day on my way home after visiting Raf, I noticed a column of black smoke as I drove around a corner nearing our home. And I knew immediately Alex had set fire to our house, and I would never see him again. I sat motionless in the car, for hours, just watching the firefighters scrambling to put the flames out, the white jets of water, the panic. Closing one eye and then the other, until the wet, charred carcass of our home finally came into focus.

Eunice Buchanan

ERIC

The Buroo wis fell busy when he got there. He tuik a deep breith. Coorse, he'd been up aa the nicht roon at Holyrood an noo his een wir strainin wi the bricht mornin sun. He wisna yuised tae daylicht. Felt maist uncomfortable.

The queue inchit forrit. '… at number five, please!' sang the voice fae the speaker for the sixth time.

For een o his bulk he wis fell licht on's feet. Een o thae stocky craturs wi feet thit walk wi a bounce an herdly seem tae touch the grund.

'Can I help you?' The wumman ahent the desk wis gaun tae be daein this for the rest o the day an had been daein it for the last twenty year. Ye cuid hear it.

'I'm no awfie shuir,' he said. 'I've been workin roon at Holyrood an it's gettin fell tedisome. I wunnert if thir wis mebbe somethin else I cuid dae.'

Vera ran a practised eye ower him. 'Have you got your P47 with you? Identification, perhaps?' She pit on her best lang-sufferin official smile. She kent the answer.

He rummlit slowly thru aa his pooches. An eence mair. Syne shuik his heid. She noddit. First score o the day. One up tae Vera.

A sma pad o white paper an a ballpoint wir plankit doon afore him. 'Write your name down here –' she tappit the pad briskly wi her pen '– and we'll see if the supervisor is available to see you.' She liftit the phone an spak a few wirds.

'Right,' she said, turnin the pad so she cuid read whit he had written, 'Mr Wight, you *are* in luck. Just go through that door there. Miss Atkins will see you now.'

As he walkit thru the door the voice fae the speaker ahent him sang, '… at number five, please!'

Miss Atkins wis sittin at a large desk. Very businesslike. Hair aa swep up at the back. Business suit. Glesses.

'Good morning, Mr Wight. Do come and sit down.' She wis awfu weel spoken.

'Come and tell me about yourself. I gather you are seeking a change of employment? Have you a job presently? Or have you been recently employed?' She luikit doon at the note that she had jist made on the pad in front o her. 'It's Eric, isn't it? May I call you Eric?' She gied him an encouragin smile.

'Aye,' he said, 'I'm jist oot o Holyrood noo. Been there aa nicht.'

'Good, good. And the work? What is your profession?' She gied him the eence ower. Herd tae say. Oot-o-the-ornar face. No likely tae be an MSP wi yon accent.

Eric reddit his thrapple an said clearly, 'I am a Bogle.'

Miss Atkins coolly tuik aff her glesses an leant forrit. 'I'm sorry, I didn't quite—'

'A Bogle. Ye ken. I fleg fowk.' He noddit, crossit ae leg ower the ither, an sat back as though that wis aa that needit tae be said.

'Mhm-mm,' said Miss Atkins. She luikit past his shuider an attemptit tae estimate hoo mony steps it wis fae her chair tae the door.

'See, I'll show ye.' He sat forrit wi his face inches fae hers an stared intae her surprisingly blue een wi tremendous concentration. He tuik a deep breith.

'Boo!'

It wis sae weak as to be nearly frichtnin in itsel. Miss Atkins cuid feel the bubble o a lauch rise in her throat. Wis this the staff haein a go at her?

He tuik a reid face an sank back luikin dishertent. 'It's nae yuise. I canna dae it in the daylicht. Some Bogles can. I canna. I need the derk.' He spak in the tone o a disappintit professional.

He rose as she stertit tae close the folder in front o her wi an air o finality. 'No!' he said. 'No! I'll show ye. I need tae get oot o the licht.' He merchit ower tae the door at the side o the room. 'Whit's this? Whit's in here?'

'That's the stationery cupboard, but—'

He graspit the haunle an turnt tae luik at her wi's eyebroos raisit. She noddit uncertainly as he held the door open.

'Jist sit quiet noo,' he said, 'an gie me a meenit or twa tae tune up. I'll show ye.' He switchit the licht on an aff again an in he went. He stuck his heid back roon the door an noddit. 'It'll dae fine,' he said. 'Jist sit there.'

She sat in the empty room an stared at the closed door to the stationery cupboard. She must be as mad as himsel. There wis no a squeak fae the cupboard. This wis daft!

Then, wi somethin like the trickle o cauld watter doon the back o her neck, she heard it. A roostle ahent her. She sat. It wis nothin. A moose. Watter in the pipes.

And again.

Then the room stertit tae chill an daurken, the blind at the winda stirred, an slowly, slowly, doon the wa under the winda, somethin black an slimy wis slidin intae the room, gaithrin wi a saft, slitherin whisper on the flair an oozin, slidin towards her. Gettin closer an closer. There wis a creak like a door openin ahent her an she froze.

'Weel, whit dae ye think?' His heid had poppit roond the door. He wis luikin fell plaised wi himsel.

The bluid stertit tae run thru her veins again. She cuid hae gien him a richt clour.

Eric stuid, haunds oot tae her, palms up, as if tae say he didna mean ony herm. 'I wis jist *showin* ye. Jist a meenit. Ye'll like this een!' He vanisht inta the cupboard eence mair.

She waitit. The room began to daurken an sheddas wir takkin shape on the back wa. Thir wis a low moanin an groanin fae the corner o the room. Suddenly there wis a large hairy Thing wi a large hairy face an large hairy haunds an it got bigger an bigger. It raisit its large hairy haunds, stuck its thoombs in its large hairy ears, wagglit its fingers at her – an' blew a resoondin raspberry.

'Coorse,' he said, comin oot o the cupboard, 'that's mair for the bairns.' She wis lauchin. It wis aa richt.

'So tell me,' she said, 'what exactly was your position – your post in Holyrood?'

'Weel, I tuik up my first position in the Palace.' He shuik his heid. 'Piece o cake. Nae self-respectin Bogle cuid fail. Aa thae derk corners an alcoves! Lamps that cast shaddas. Great heavy doors that wid gie ye a creak tae die for!' He wis well inta a rapture o recollection. 'Wuid panels tae tap! Curtains tae shoogle!'

He slumpt onta the chair, jist a picter o the sair-hertit.

'Tell me, Eric,' Miss Atkins sat forrit wi her elbas on the table and askit, in an effort tae distract him, 'What is it all about? Why do you have to give someone a fright – a – a – fleg? Is it just for fun?'

'Fun? Fun?' His bushy eyebroos drew thegither. For a meenit she thocht she micht hae offendit him. 'Aye, weel, I hae tae admit there *is* an element o that. We hae a richt lauch whiles, back at the workshops an seminars.'

Her expression registert a certain amount o surprise.

'Och, aye,' he said, 'I'm daein my Maister's noo. I've duin aa the theory an noo I hae the practical.' He thocht for a meenit. 'I suppose it maun be like the dentists. Ye cuidna let them loose wi thir dreels an pliers wi'oot ony previous instruction. An a bit o supervised practice.'

Eric sat back an made himsel mair comfortable. 'Onywey, fun? Aye, weel. Ye'll hae been up the Royal Mile? Aye. Hauntit hooses. Ghost walks. An whit are they sellin like the proverbial hot bannocks? Flegs!'

She noddit slowly. 'I must admit, Eric, I have never thought of it quite like that.'

'I tell ye,' said he, draain his chair forrit, 'jist you buy an auld hoose wi a cellar an employ a Bogle tae blaw a chill air in the back bedroom an moan a bit – ye're in the money! Fowk *like* tae be fleggit.'

He cuid see she still wisna convinced.

'Look at aa thae fowk claain thir wey up rock faces or peyin guid money tae jump aff the Forth Brig tied on wi a bit o elastic? Whit aboot them, eh? We had it aa gaun inta by the Pheesiology Professor in oor second year. When ye get a fleg, he says, ye get a kick fae th' adrenaline that heezes up yer hert an gies yer hale corpus an upsteer. Syne when it's ower ye feel that gled tae survive that ye're set up for the week.' He gied her a wee wink. 'I cuid tell ye felt gey briskent up yersel efter yer wee fleg.'

Miss Atkins' cheeks reidit. She smoothit back an imaginary stray hair an tidied the papers in front o her.

'What about your work now, Mr Wight – Eric? Do I take it that you are no longer employed at Holyrood?'

'Nae langer at the Palace,' said Eric. 'I've been shiftit ower the wey tae the Parliament. It wis,' he said modestly but wi a certain satisfaction, 'a wee step up the ladder. My supervisor suggestit I try somethin wi a bit mair challenge.'

He pu'd his chair closer an spak quiet-like. 'There is anither side tae the effects o fear, that they're luikin inta.' He sat back. 'I'm shuir ye're awfu busy. Am I takkin up yer time, Miss –' his een slid sideweys tae the sma notice on her desk '– Atkins?'

She had become that fascinated by the movement o his eyebroos that the direct question tuik her by surprise. 'Not at all. No. No. Do carry— Call me Gladys.'

'Richt – Gladys. It's weel kent that the biggest stride forrit in man's mental capacity cam in the Steen Age,' Eric wis getting inta his stride noo an wis fell awa wi himsel, 'when he had tae hae een in the back o's heid for aa the terrors presentit wi mammoths an bears an sabre-tooth tigers an – aa thon. An him wi only souple wit an bare haunds tae keep him richt.'

Miss Atkins – Gladys – wis spellbound.

'I'm no talkin aboot the lang-staunin wearisome fears or sensible fears. I'm talkin aboot *flegs*. Wee shots o fricht that catch ye like a tingle o static electricity – that stob the brain an activate the neurons like laldie. Noo, the depairtment had a lecture fae a Kobold-Meister fae een o the colleges in Bavaria. He's been workin on the effect o flegs on the development o the brain. In fact, he has produced, ower a period o years, a number o weel-respeckit papers. Some o us students hae been set up tae test the hypotheesis that flegs, properly regulatit an administert ower a set period o time, raise the IQ by a significant number o points.'

He stoppit an regardit her wi raised broos. 'Are ye still wi me?'

Gladys cuid only nod.

'Ye hae tae understaund that whit he is sayin is that flegs dinna jist get ye kittlit up temporarily but that neural pathways are creatit an ye end up an awfu lot mair lang-heidit – mair up tae snuff, as ye micht say.'

Eric paused.

Gladys rose an indicatit the tray wi its bonny lace doyley an denty teacups. 'Would you care for a cup of tea, Eric? This is absolutely fascinating.' She was switching the kettle on as she spak. 'Please, do go on.'

'Weel, the idea wis for me tae move oot o Holyrood Palace whaur I wis daein my trainin an set this up in the Parliament biggin an see if it works.' He stoppit an pit his haund ower his mou. 'I shuidna really be tellin ye this. Thir no supposed to ken! Ye'll no mention it, will ye?

It's no easy tae gie fowk a fleg if thir expeckin it.' He shuik his finger at her an gied a wee lauch. 'Ye're jist awfu easy tae talk tae.'

She smiled modestly. 'Do you take milk, Eric?'

He went on, 'That's jist aboot it – except for ae ither thing that's mair difficult tae deal wi, although the Parapsychology Department here hae been ettlin tae get at it for years. Aye, jist the ae sugar, please.'

He spak slowly an seriously as he steerit his tea. 'On the question o whit lies ahent it aa, I ken nae mair than ony ither body. What lies oot o sicht an maks sic things possible, I dinna ken. But what we, in the department, hae come tae see is, that sometimes, a knowledge o somethin "ither" that ye dinna understaund – that wee sense o unease – is enough tae mak ye stop an mind that ye dinna ken aathin. Ye micht come tae mak yer decisions wi a bit mair circumspection.'

She leant forrit wi the plate o biscuits. He wis stertin tae soond fell dowie again.

'Onywey,' he went on, 'we wir aa set up tae luik at that eence we got goin in the Parliament buildings an I jist felt that I had let aabody doon. Cuidna raise a whustle.'

He tuik a sip o tea an pit doon his jaffa cake. 'The lichtin's aa wrang an aabody's bustlin aboot luikin busy. That's aa ye need – owerheid lichtin an bustle! I cuidna hack it. When I cam in here I wis that scunnert I wis ready tae gie the hale thing the elba.'

He tuik anither sip syne, gied a wee cough an said, 'I wid jist like tae say that ye hae been awfu kind an I feel mair like masel noo.'

'Not at all, Eric. That's what we're here for. Tell me,' she said shyly, 'can anyone be trained to do what you do? To be a Bogle?'

He pit doon his cup. 'Weel, I aye think it's a bit like music. Near aabody can learn tae play a penny whustle but we're no aa Mozart. Ye dinna get on the course wi'oot demonstratin yer innate ability. How wir ye askin?'

Gladys luikit doon an shufflit the papers on the table. 'Well,' she said, 'I don't know whether it would be relevant, but I have had some success with reading the tea-leaves.'

Eric rose smertly tae his feet. 'Richt,' he said, 'we can soon find oot. I'll tell ye whit tae dae. Ye need tae tak my haund. When I hae got goin – if my manifestations are increased by your innate power – then we'll ken for shuir.'

He cuid see she wis fell conflummixt by these technical terms. 'Ye see, it will be your pooer addit tae mine. Sae gin ye hae the makkins o a Bogle, the twa o us thegither will be shuir tae get some ootlandish ferlies.'

Gladys wis up like a shot.

Eric studied the licht an the blind. 'It'll hae tae be the cupboard,' he said. 'Ye'll need tae tak aff the jaiket. The metal buttons. Micht hae iron. It raivels the magnetic field.' He luikit doon at her feet. 'An the shuin. Thae buckles. Turn roond. Aye, thae preens in yer hair. Oot wi them.' His voice wis deep an very masterfu.

'Ye'll tak my haund,' he said, 'an we'll need tae sit awfu quiet in the dark whilst I get under wey.'

She held oot her haund. Inta the cupboard they went. An shut the door.

Noo they must hae been sittin awfu quiet seence, when Vera knockit on the door an cam in tae see if Miss Atkins wis ready for her veesitors, thir wis naebody tae be seen, an, thocht Vera, yon Mr Wight maun hae slippit oot wi'oot her noticin him.

Sae it was, that jist as the Provost an the Heid Pilliedacus o Social Services wir being shown in, they cuid aa hear strange moanin soonds comin fae the stationery cupboard accompanied by unexpectit bumps an roostlins. That wis when they spottit the jaikit flung ower the back o the chair, the kickit-aff shuin an the mysterious puckle preens on the table.

Syne wi a sudden ootburst o delichtit lauchter the cupboard door wis flung wide an the pair o them sailed oot tae be confrontit by officialdom – her barefit an reid-cheekit wi excitement, wi her bonny blonde hair tummilt aboot her shuiders.

And, as Vera telt her freends later, nane the twa o them ae bit abashit. The last she saw o them they wir aff doon the road haund in haund an luikin fell vauntie.

Sinsyne they hae been hingin aboot roon the debatin chamber at Holyrood, jist sussin it oot. The project is no richt stertit but, as Eric said tae his supervisor, 'Eence we hae mappit oot oor parameters an adjustit oor combined wattage tae gravitational an magnetic influences – there shuid be plenty scope.'

Jim Carruth

CHECKING OUT THE DEER

My wife was glad that I wasn't there
when our car hit a doe on the old road
glanced it, legs akimbo, onto the verge.
She's sure I would've made a meal of it
for that's what my kind do with words
picking away at its still warm carcass,
ruminating on the spirit and death.

And if the car had been full of poets
she would've kept the child locks on
as she went back to check the animal
holding their morbid fascinations at bay,
salivating and panting dogs in the heat,
each palm slapping against the window
a tiny troubled songbird trapped inside.

Defne Çizakça

HAGOP'S FIRST NIGHT OF STORYTELLING

You choose your storyteller like you choose a lover. I picked Hayalci as my teacher because he has a face you would cross mountains and seas to find. When he is calm, his brown eyes are flecked with honey, full of gentleness and love. The listeners see a father in him. And yet, I can envisage with certainty, my storyteller is a fierce lover too. Once he becomes curious, his gaze is filled with passion, and violence, and a wish to divine mysteries. I am trying to learn the depths and the heights of his imagination; I want to chart him like a landscape.

The coffeehouse in which I live has been on the same spot since 1555, snug between the church of Aya Pantelemion and the big oak tree. The scribes before me have placed the coffeehouse books in a rosewood chest with three visible locks, and one that is invisible. I sew sachets of lavender against the moths and worms, round my neck I hide the four keys that unfasten the books, and every evening I listen to the storyteller in hopes of a new tale.

The first scribe in this coffeehouse had the initial book and the clear pages. From the records I see he listened to the story of 'Black Mustafa the Hero'. I can picture him before my eyes: he sits at the back of the room and notes down every word the storyteller utters. As he writes he smokes a *çubuk*; he inhales deep and the smoke does not leave him till the story halts. He laughs with the audience, and he cries. Because he has filled our first book centuries ago, his words are the norm and the truth. We only note down derivations and irregularities: how storyteller Yusuf embellished the ending of 'Keloğlan', how Yakup got rid of the prince in 'The Bird of Sorrow', how Kız Ismail narrated 'The Imp of the Well' from back to front the night Sultan Abdülaziz died. I have arrived very late; this coffeehouse has a memory of three hundred years and more. The stories in it are tattered.

There are two things I do each night, once all the customers have left. The first is that I unlock the leather book to make side notes, *derkenar*, on a story already written down. I need to be picky with what I choose to write, need to remember all the coffeehouse books prior to mine so that I don't repeat the scribes who came before me. This is hard work and requires discipline, double-checking, and submission to the slow torment of my profession. Sometimes I add a word, sometimes only a comma. My fastidiousness is why Ioannis Efendi trusts the keys of the rosewood chest to me.

The second thing I do every night, and which is forbidden, is that I am slowly writing a book no one else knows about. I fill it with the tales that make up my storyteller's life.

The book of Hayalci is made of cardboard and yellow, crisp parchment – that is all I could afford. Its pages fall apart because my hands are not expert at stitching. I made it when Ioannis Efendi lay asleep, and I light a candle to write in it only when he begins to snore. One day the pages under my fingertips will guide me to tell my own tales, in this very coffeehouse, and it is out of the same book that I will make a map of Hayalci's thoughts.

Night One

The days in the coffeehouse start slow but finish late. Customers begin to trickle in around noon and from then on until night-time there is constant backgammon, and chess, and money exchanging hands under the table, and the homeless dozing off in the warmth of the braziers, and the rich traders, and the poor porters and in short anyone who can afford a cup of coffee comes in here. But only those who stay until dark enter it to sustain their souls. They come to open their *kısmet*. Because Allah is the best storyteller, and Hayalci the second best.

It was the twelfth of Zilhicce – a night of rain, a night of confusion – when a heavy man entered the premises and unsettled our sheltered rhythms. The sash around his fez was red, indicating he was Christian, the coat he wore was European but old and missing a few buttons. The stranger had a worn face with deep wrinkles like knife slashes. When he entered the coffeehouse the empty seats filled up. The regulars knew, from the way he walked into the coffeehouse, that they would not like this man.

The first person he talked to was Hayalci. He took my storyteller by the arm and asked whether he could tell the story this evening. An unusual calm imbued his request; my teller halted for only a second in which the stranger stepped on to the table where the chair was placed – the throne of the storyteller – and took Hayalci's place.

'*Ey ahali*,' he began, 'I know you are here to listen to the storyteller but you will listen to me tonight.' His voice was crackling and low. 'If you don't like what I tell after the first break, I will not return to your coffeehouse.' The man in the red sash waited for possible opposition, and when none was voiced he adjusted the velvet cushion for comfort. Someone in the back must have known him. The customers whispered from ear to ear, and that is how I learned the new teller's name was Hagop.

'The story is long and might take a couple of nights to tell. If you like it we may be together for a while. I promise not to tell you anything that is not true; reason enough for you to stay and listen, if you ask me. I know for a fact, most tales told on this table are either made up or complete lies.

'There are many ways I can tell you of my life. One is through the theatre; I used to own one. Lately I have a habit of sitting alone wherever I go: coffeehouse, *hamam*, whorehouse, graveyard ... but it wasn't always like that. It may not look like it now, but I used to have money – a lot of it – and then there was a time I didn't have any at all.

'I can also start with Kasturya. Some of you know the neighbourhood, but none of you can imagine the violence in its cobblestoned streets. The madhouses underneath its churches, the secret night-time burials, the fear of the *khabadayi*.

'Or I can start from the middle of a love story. I am thirty-eight years old and handsome, so they used to tell me. I lie in bed, remembering my past as if it had been centuries in the making: my childhood as stalker, my adulthood as rope walker, and everything in between which I have kept secret until now. I know Nora is watching me through the mirror. As I drift off, the heat of her gaze is on my skin, on the tips of my fingers, and I wonder if I can make her love me again.'

Hagop paused. He looked at the men listening to him, took a long minute, stared even into my eyes. I felt uncomfortable, both from his gaze and from his way of telling. Neither was proper. I wanted to inform him it was not tasteful to start from the midst of a story; we are taught not to cut a tale open with a knife. One must start slow and caressing, like you would start with a woman. A run and a riddle takes the audience away from the real world, it warms them up for the listening, nurtures them curious. Still, the biggest mistake Hagop made that first night was not his rush, but his indecision.

The storyteller must know, before he starts the telling, why and where and how the tale will begin and how and why and where it will end. He can only change details during the narration, subtract a day or two, add a minor character, a few side stories. He can hide some small truth, or reveal a random secret, perhaps postpone revelations. But if a teller has many ways to tell a story, he has not understood its meaning. The first thing a scribe learns from his storyteller is that a good tale chooses how it wants to be told. Accordingly, my expectations of the man with the missing buttons were low, and yet I listened.

That first night, the audience and I listened to Hagop for more than three coffee breaks. Even the stingy customers paid him *bahşiş* so that he continue. I think he lured us in with that one sentence. Most of the stories told on this table were indeed made up, or a bunch of lies. That was our age-old tradition. And there was something arousing, as well as terrible, about the possibility of a true story. Something arousing and terrible about a man who would only tell the truth.

And so our unwinding began on the night we met Hagop. It was a stormy darkness in the month of Zilhicce – a night of rain, a night of confusion – and the first time I had the clear pages. The first occasion in my life where I got to write down a story that had never been told before.

Polly Clark

WYSTAN COMES TO HELENSBURGH, EASTER 1930

His jacket is tweed with a herringbone stitch on it, a kind of winter green, and rather too large. The lining has come loose and a button is hanging by a thread, destined to drop before the train reaches Birmingham. Beneath the jacket, a grey shirt and a spotted tie. The shirt has a greasy stain down the front. His arms are huge, the arms of an ape, and he's lighting a cigarette as he gets settled for the journey from Oxford to Glasgow. Oiled or greasy, it's hard to tell, his hair is close shaved at the back and sides, with a fringe hanging louchely over his forehead. His left ear sticks out, the remains of the schoolboy, but his face is lined already. The impression made is one of pale, large fragility.

It isn't until he looks up that his attractiveness becomes apparent. His blue eyes flicker with a lively intelligence that animates all his features. It's as if one can see the thoughts playing in his mind. But this is an illusion: his friends will find they never really know him. Wystan is that terrible isolating thing, *unreadable*. His hands are enormous, dwarfing the matchbox. He holds it gently, a giant lifting a farmhouse.

Every few minutes he has to get up and walk around. He is recovering from an operation for an anal fissure, and it is still, after many weeks, unbearably painful to sit down. Though its refusal to heal is depressing him, he has started to consider the intimate, searing pain as a physical expression of the torment he feels all the time, which is sutured into his very biology. The wound that will not heal, that cannot be spoken of in polite company, is becoming a separate entity. He composes, idly in his head, as the train clatters along, a letter to the Wound. He wants to make peace with it. He wants to be forgiven.

There are two others in his carriage: a suited man whose bowler hat is neatly on the rack above, and a man with a florid face, sour with drink, who has fallen asleep against the window. The purple of his mouth is visible as he snores. Wystan studies them in between glancing at the pages of the *Criterion*. The two destinies of Man. Suited looks well fed and contented. He is reading the financial information at the back of the paper, and his face has an ageing softness that denotes a life free of depravity. Florid radiates ill health from every broken capillary. No wife, no children, no love. In time, Wystan is surely to become one of these men. Once we are all grown up, there is nothing else.

Wystan is going to be a Great Poet. He has decided it firmly, told all his friends. His philosophy of life is inspired by Emile Coué: you will become what you believe you will become. Eighteen months ago he graduated from Oxford after a sensational three years, but with a very poor degree, and T. S. Eliot has, that very week, accepted his manuscript for publication. He lets his cigarette glow in his fingers and stares as the train hauls itself out of Coventry station and continues the drag and choke to Scotland.

His work is not where his doubts lie; that is not what draws his gaze nervously to Florid snuffling before him. It is love. He shuffles in his seat to relieve the pressure on the Wound. It pulsates with its own torn language, telling him that he will never really know love.

Wystan rubs his white brow, pushes his fringe out of his eyes and rummages in his satchel, swapping the *Criterion* for a book. He's reading a lot of Freud at this time; it offers him little comfort.

Sheilagh snaps into his mind, her pretty frown causing him a pang. When he proposed to her, he was confident that even if he was not in love, then he would be soon. She had accepted in the bemusing way women had of being excited about invisible things, and he found her endearing. Sheilagh was a nurse, and she brought that feminine practicality to their relationship. She knew about bodies, so he did not feel the need to be the oracle in this area, and she also knew about the way things are meant to be. Best of all, Sheilagh was nothing like his mother, which was certainly progress, for he deemed much of his problem to be his excessive attachment to his domineering mother. He was twenty-two at the time, surely old enough to know his own mind.

But then she started crying, quite soon into it all. She was disappointed in him, without saying why. Before this, Wystan had, quite simply, never been a disappointment, and this had not played well with him.

Hills swell beyond the window and a few drops of rain spatter the glass. The whistle blares at Carlisle station, doors slam, and Florid jolts awake, glares round at his companions before reaching into his bag and unwrapping a packet of sandwiches. Wystan is interested in the sandwiches. They have been neatly wrapped in paper and tied with string. Who has done this for Florid? A wife? A mother? Has he perhaps done it himself? The smell of egg fills the carriage. Sniffing, the man reaches into his bag again and pulls out a bottle of beer. He flicks off the cap with a penny and sets it between his knees. Suited looks sideways with a detached sort of sneer. The conductor, a half-pint man in a scarlet livery, appears in the doorway.

'Which way is the bar?' asks Wystan. He forgot about lunch, and didn't really appreciate how long the journey is. The conductor points backwards. 'Two coaches down, sir.' He looks at his watch. 'Still a few ham sandwiches I believe.' Wystan nods. In a while he'll wander up to the bar and see what there is. He sighs and observes through the window the almost imperceptible change in the greens and browns of Cumbria to those of Dumfriesshire.

The London establishment, which waits both to claim and judge him in a few years, shrinks to a speck. He is coming, for as long as they'll have him, to the briny shores, the promenade of hardware shops and grimy cafes; to the land of shallow valleys and low hills, of violet summers. He is coming to the land of naval ships, with its seething hatred of outsiders, with its petty religious tyrannies. Soon he will drop submarines casually into his poems; the sea will creep into his soul.

It's not his choice exactly. His trust money is about to run out, and he needs a job. His friend Cecil Day-Lewis has nominated him for this post of schoolmaster at Larchfield school, though he has no experience of teaching and a severe distrust of the school environment. Florid coughs over his beer, drains it and fishes another out of his bag. Suited shakes his newspaper, expertly rolls it up and slips it under his arm before leaving the carriage, presumably to go to the bar. Wystan says, 'Shall I open the window?' and Florid grunts his assent. Cool Scottish air rushes in. Florid's hands are trembling. The sole of one boot is coming adrift and his laces are undone. Wystan knows he would rather end up as Florid than Suited, and indeed that is his trajectory. There's an honesty about Florid. He's given up trying to be what he is not.

When Sheilagh told Wystan his poems disgusted her, he knew that wasn't *it*, or wasn't it exactly. Her intuition that his poems were not about her, or anything she'd recognise, was certainly correct, but as she sat sobbing into her hands he wondered if he should press her to tell him what it was. At that moment he hated her enough to humiliate them both. He might say *so let's talk about disgust then* and see if it led to a conversation with any honesty in it. In truth, she bored rather than disgusted him; her body bored him, her deference bored him. Most of all her safety bored him, even while he craved it. Should he tell her all this?

And yet, she loved him. On his side there had certainly been hope, massive, tremendous hope. And is hope not the sibling of love? She wanted him to apologise for the poems in some way, to deny that what she thought was in them was in them. He couldn't do that, but he could apologise for himself.

Which he did. He cried while he did it, and he held her hand until he had finished. *Not cut out for marriage. You deserve someone better. A proper man.* She didn't look up when he left. When he reached home he went to bed, where relief crashed over him and he cried until he was empty.

Wound is communicating its discomfort. Wystan gets up to walk to the bar. Why should this journey put him so in mind of Sheilagh? Perhaps he knows that after her there will be no love of the kind he wants. He has chosen the Wound over healing. The train sways as if nodding its assent. Wystan feels suddenly tearful and digs his nails into his palm. Anyway, now is a new beginning. He could barely be further from Sheilagh and the hopes he had of change.

Wystan is going to the heartland of – as he will soon describe it – the enemy. He feels unruffled, physical discomfort notwithstanding. It has all been decided. He will live quietly, teaching English and French to the sons of Scotchmen and he will get on with his work. He will be able to establish his routine for writing, he will be able to devote himself to it. Provided, of course, that he causes no scandals.

Terese Coe

BREAKING IT DOWN

The holy that is mad
the hopeful in the had
the dragon in the bird
the two that are a third
the brother in the foe
the drought in the overflow

the child's play in the skill
a hotspot in the chill
the inertia in the spin
the death-throe in the grin
the certainty of maybe
the dead man in the baby

Stewart Conn

FRAGMENTS

Breakage

On its hook in the kitchen is the largest fragment
of the mug you clutched as you fell, smaller pieces
on the worktop. Hard to imagine them fitting together,
their fractures knitting, far less reinstating the whole –
so intricate a task, time and patience needed. Yet
nothing to the near-miracle required, to render
your happiness, the lives we share, recoverable.

Sunflowers

In a photo taken a couple of days before your
fall, you are dwarfed by two sunflowers potted
last spring, casting dark shadows against our wall.
The sunflowers shrivel now, their prime over,
while what you must do is grow tall … grow tall.

In Your Room

Against banked pillows, all swansdown,
supported by a metal headrest, you look

for all the world like a sleeping princess
from a fairy tale, not in a glass case, but

dosages of medication and painkillers
sustaining you under duress. If only

I were that prince whose kiss could
provide instant and magical release.

Gordon Dargie

THE SHIFT

A miner on the bus adjusts his coat
and this permits the boy to sit beside him

and miners' faces see that he can sit
or go on standing. They are quiet with coal.

Just mind an keep yer claes, the miner says
and leaves him to fit in, the calculations

shifting on the corners, approximate
but still you don't look round when miners manage

home the way they are and people come to terms
with honest dirt that by the end will kill

his grandfather but it is not his place
to bring that up, among the coal faces

that open in bright lines where they were gathered.

Anne Donovan

OUR NELSON

The tar stuck tae the soles of wur shoes it was that hot. The march went on for miles, couldnae see the endy it.

Yer da was behind me. His daft pal kept makin stupit jokes but he was dead quiet.

Too busy lookin at that red hair of yours. Doon tae her waist so it was. Glintin in the sun.

Ah've heard it a million times, story of how they met. Ah smile, tune oot.

*

Nelson was like an uncle or a cousin who lived far away, wanny the family. Any time his name was mentioned, the TV was turnt up; Mammy cut photies and articles oot the paper, kept them in a folder. The stories were endless – how they'd went on the marches tae free him, rummled through oranges and grapefruits in the shops tae make sure they didnae come fae South Africa. Ma folks knew the words of 'Nkosi Sikelel' iAfrika' better than 'Auld Lang Syne'.

And their best story was the day he came.

*

It was chuckin it. Kinda rain you think is gonnae wear itsel oot, cannae last. But it did.

We were there dead early, got right tae the front, just at the barriers. Drookit, so we were. You couldnae put up an umbrella it was that crowded.

Waited two hours for him.

Would of waited for ever.

He was that close, just yards away.

Mind the singin?

And when he started dancin? Magic.

Second-best day of ma life, son. Apart fae havin you.

Thanks, Ma.

*

There's a photie of them on that day, framed, pride of place among the family weddings, christenings and first communions. Efter he'd left the square they wandered aboot, in a dwam, ma da said, nae clue where they were gaun; a journalist asked them for their thoughts and a photographer snapped them for the paper.

Ah tellt him, says ma da. *We were the first city tae make him a free man, when he was still in thon jail. Hauf the time they act like a bunch a eejits in the council, but we should be proud of Glasgow for daein that. They never printed it but. Never even put wur names in.*

Ma smiles. *They published the photie but.*

They look that young, haudin haunds in the rain, hair plastered tae their heids, eyes shinin. It had just started tae dry up and the grey streets glistered.

Like a monsoon it was.

But efter the rain, the rainbow nation.

*

Ma and Da got engaged that day.

Ah was too feart tae ask her afore, says ma da. *Scared of gettin tied doon, ah guess. But somehow, efter that day, ah knew it was the right thing for us. He gied me the courage.*

There's a lot of talk like this, aboot the things that matter, since ma da's been sick. It's like he's tryin tae cram it all in.

They werenae sure at first but they operated on him a month ago and noo there's nae doubt. Ma's tryin tae get him hospice care but they have tae get his lung drained afore he can leave the ward. She's always wi him; her work's been great, gied her the time. Ah'm there too, except when ah've got a class at the uni.

*

It's the day efter Nelson's passing. Da looks at the photies in the paper, gets me tae read out the articles, smilin at the quotes. There's a bit about Glasgow, how they named a street efter him.

That caused a right stushie, says ma mammy.

They're havin a gatherin for him there at five o'clock the night.

Ma and Da look at each other.

It's four noo, son, he says, his voice a hoarse whisper. *You could make it easy. Pay wur respects.*

Ah want tae stay here wi you.

Last few days they've been flexible wi the visitin; Ma and me stay on till they come round wi the meals, grab a bite in the cafe then back to the ward.

A cough racks his thin body; Ma gies him tissues, strokes his back. When he recovers, he squeezes ma haund. *Dae it fur me, son.*

*

It's a bitter night, cauld dampness seepin through yer bones. They've set up a kinda tent thing and are playin African music as the crowd gathers. Some folk are wavin scarves and dancin but maist are sombre. A guy's talkin aboot Nelson, and all he done – the same stories ah've heard fae ma folks. He's a good guy, the speaker, fought against apartheid since the sixties.

Viva Mandela!

Viva! we shout.

It's even caulder noo. The crowd has thickened, we're closer thegether, a ragbag of ages and colours: folk smart fae offices or trauchled wi Christmas parcels. They're shufflin aboot on the wee stage and somebody else is talkin. Then another. Too much talkin. Ah thought we'd be silent, light candles, remember him. Ah'm gettin twitchy noo. Ah turn, start tryin tae fight ma way back through the huddle of folk when ma phone goes, as ah knew it would, and the text is fae ma mammy, as ah knew it would be.

Ah staund at the bus stop, think on all the times the three of us had been thegether. Why was ah at this haund-knitted gatherin insteidy wi my da? Ah should of just stayed at the hospital, ah should of been there.

Ah get on the bus, climb up the stair and sit in the front seat lookin out at the dreich night. The rain has smeared the windaes and they gleam in the streetlights. Ah mind the picture of my folks on that second-best day of their lives.

Dae it fur me, son.

Carol Farrelly

THE ROOFTOP BUSKER

Askrigg, July 1947

I grip heel to tile: I find my balance. A pair of slim white doves dart between my legs. They navigate me as part of this rooftop, a chimney, weathered but stable. And already they glide across the village square towards the church spire, circle once, and continue westwards. I watch them recede, two ghost children, holding hands. I find my smile, raise my violin and look to my audience below.

Wedding guests mill across the sun-speckled square. A waltz, perhaps, might please them: they seem traditional sorts, from the little I've gleaned of the folk in these parts. A liking for meat cased in pastry, and pale ales, and music that will roll out green hills before them and return to them a world most fear lost – and some know lost. I angle my bow.

A pot-bellied man and his wife walk beneath me, towards the inn door. They stop by the foot of my ladder. A black terrier cavorts behind and between and before them. They stare now at the sign I've strung to the third rung: 'Rooftop busker. Please donate.' The man looks up, nudges the woman, crooks his walking stick and points at me. They both stare. The dog stares too. Folk often do. In the villages and towns I've passed through these last months, they often pause on their daily journeys to the butcher or the cemetery or the office and they marvel. I've coaxed rooftop pitches from teashop owners, grocers and even vicars, either marrying or burying. My violin brushes kinder colours into their bones and mortar and they want that. We all want that, now.

I smile, angle my bow again and prepare for the glorious friction of grease and string. A waltz will settle them. And there, in a blink, behind the plump couple, the small, blonde boy appears again. He's right on cue. Third day in a row.

My bow falters. He stares. Each day he has come and watched and listened, once in the company of a white-haired man and yesterday and today alone. And he unnerves me. Children don't usually unnerve me. They are usually the more curious and generous, keen to climb my ladder and weight my purple cap with pennies or sixpence or the odd shilling. And they all remark on the wonder of the idea as they let the coins fall. 'A rooftop busker!' they say. Sometimes they comment on the one purple glove I wear. 'Helps my hold,' I tell them. It is this boy's reserve that unnerves me: he watches but he never comes to give. He senses the undeserving in me.

The man and woman shrug and smile and wander inside. Their terrier follows. The boy stays, but a stocky figure stands behind him now, all braces and pear-shaped belly. He pats the boy's head with a sun-brown hand.

'All right, sir?' he shouts up.

This rooftop is his, the landlord. A jovial man, he lets me busk and, in return, reckons on drawing 'a fair few more pints than normal' from his pumps.

I nod down at him and position my bow yet again. 'On top of the world!'

'We're about ready for a few tunes, sir!' he says. 'The bride and groom's feet are a-itching now!' He squeezes the boy's shoulder as he speaks. 'As are little Tom's feet.'

On top of the world, I repeat to myself. On top. Always wandering. Never staying. Never itching.

'Of course,' I say.

I begin to count down. Today's bride, he told me earlier, is a young widow. 'Her husband fell at Monte Cassino. Poor bugger. She's marrying his older brother,' he said. I nodded, sipped on my ale, knew nothing to say. 'He'll make a good father to her little girl. They're blood, after all.' I smiled and still said nothing. My brother left me nothing and nobody to tend. No wife. No child. Not even a grave.

'A waltz, is it?' the landlord shouts.

I pull the bow and draw a note and a magpie lands on the guttering. It tilts a glossy eye towards the cap by my feet and it clucks. I pause. If it dive-bombs, I'll snatch the cap quicker than its beak can. Magpies are the flimsiest, flappiest of bombers and they only drop slops of white shit. They don't torch roofs or wither houses into black ruins.

The magpie nods its head, turns and flaps westwards.

I count myself down again. 'One, two, one–two–three—'

A pair of small white hands curl around the gutter. The blonde-haired boy grins at me, blushing from ear to ear. He has finally come.

'I'm Tomek,' he says, in an accent I can't place. 'But you can call me Tom, if you prefer. That's what most people call me here.'

I say nothing.

'What's your name?' he asks, still smiling.

'Jack,' I answer, peering over his head. The landlord below is talking to the groom and they're both shuddering laughter. The bride is crouching on the cobbles before her little girl and wiping her cheek.

'Jack for Jacob?' he asks. 'Or Jacques? Or Jakub?'

'Just Jack,' I say.

He shrugs and then he rattles stories at me for five minutes. He tells me he moved here only last year with his grandparents. He's eleven, he says, although everyone thinks he looks younger. His English, so everyone tells him, is very good, if a little 'soft and Southern-sounding'. He tilts his head, like the magpie, to see if I might agree. I smile and shrug back. He comes, he says, from a very pretty village in southern Poland.

'So pretty,' he says. 'Like this village. Except our roofs are better. We have more colours in our roofs.'

The violin is growing sticky in my left, ungloved hand. I lay it down between the steps on the small ladder I've laid flat on the tiles. The bride and groom can wait another minute.

'Poland's a beautiful country,' I say.

His eyes darken. 'You know it?'

I crouch down on the tiles, so I'm nearer his eye level.

'Well, it looks beautiful in the pictures I've seen.'

It's true. I've seen photographs since, in the newspapers. Anyone can see those towns were once beautiful. And Ralf said so, in the one letter he sent home. So many church spires, he said.

Tomek grins and hands me a penny, hot from his grasping fingers. He prods it into my gloved hand.

'And you?' he asks. 'Where are you from? Everybody in the village's wondering.'

'Are they now?'

Folk can never place my accent. They often ask and I always give the same answer: 'a little-known crater, the other side of the moon'. Sometimes they smile and give up; other times they frown and walk away, suddenly wiping their perfectly dry hands.

'I'm a bit of a mongrel,' I add. 'Best way to be.'

'Mongrel?' His dark eyes squint through a net of sunlight. 'Where is Mongrel?'

I laugh. 'I'm from across the sea. The continent.'

'You escaped here too?'

I swallow and shake my head. I should have brought a drink up here with me.

He nuzzles his chin against the gutter, as though he means to settle for a while. I glance over his shoulder. The wedding folk will be pining for music now and the landlord growing impatient. No adults, however, wait below. No bride and groom. No landlord. No white-haired man as on the first day. His absence since is strange. The grandfather, perhaps. Usually, the parent or older sibling or grandparent stands at the bottom of the ladder, either cooing words of ascent to the child or following them, cocooning them with arms and breath. It's always a beautiful sight.

'Here,' I say. 'How about looking at your new English home from up here? A bird's-eye view?'

He nods and grabs at the rooftop ladder. As he steps onto the tiles, he looks back to the ground below, tilting his head in the smallest movements as though balancing a book.

'You're safe,' I murmur and I anchor my hands to his shoulders.

He turns to face the market cross and the church.

'The cross –' he points and laughs, 'it is like two matchsticks.'

'I suppose it is.'

'And the gravestones,' he says, quieter. 'They are sleeping birds, all folded.'

I squeeze his shoulder. I used to see such things too as a child.

'Now look beyond the village,' I say. 'Look down the dale and up the hill. Have you ever seen such shades of green and gold?'

'And blue,' he replies.

'Blue undertones, yes. You've an artist's eye.'

He glances up at me, no blush of pride on his cheeks. 'Is it because of so much rain here? It makes the grass and trees have blue?'

'Maybe,' I smile. 'Now see that limestone terrace over there? The hard flat stone rising higher than all the other land, reaching up into the sky? Isn't that a piece of magnificence? So resilient.'

'Re-si-li-ent.' He tests out the word. 'You mean like the quiet people praying in church?'

'What?'

'The people thanking God. Resilient.'

I shake my head. 'I think you mean reverent.'

He smiles. 'Ah, that's my word.'

'Resilient is different. Resilient means strong. The stone over there is stronger than in other parts and that's why it survives – why it stands taller and higher. It can fight off the wind and rain.'

He frowns and folds his arms. 'No need. There's no need to fight any more.'

'The land always fights.'

'No more fighting. Not for us. That's what my granddad says. No more fighting or hiding. Now we can work. And get paid. And eat and sleep.'

I rub his shoulder. I might say such simple things too, if I ever have children and grandchildren. I'd tell the kindest lies to my children's children. Never again, I would say. No more fighting. Humans are different from the earth. No need to admire limestone. And when I come home at night, I would lift my violin and brush colours reminiscent of sun into our walls and cushions and beds.

'No more hiding,' he repeats.

'No,' I whisper.

I look at the back of his small neck and wonder how much he saw of the war in Poland. Perhaps the parents he hasn't mentioned, or his grandfather, protected him. They took him down roads that avoided any glimpse of wet ghetto roofs; they crossed over borders in cat-soft silence; they muffled his ears to the drill of gunfire and any rumour of the camps. They managed, perhaps, where the rest of us failed. They kept a child intact.

'Look at the pilot birds,' he points.

'Swallows.'

'They float above the ...' He falters. 'How did you say?'

'The terrace.'

'They float like you float on the roof.' He twists his blonde head to look back up at me, grinning, showing a gap in his lower teeth. The next moment, he reaches down and pats my scuffed shoe. His fingers catch on a lace and his left foot stumbles. I grab him by the neck, as a pup.

'Tomek!' a man shouts.

We both look down. The white-haired man stands at the foot of the ladder, staring up, his arms raised wide in the pose of a priest blessing the communion bread.

Tomek ducks his head. 'He wants me to come down.'

'Your granddad?' I loosen my hold on him.

'He says you're a magician.'

'Yes, music's a magic, of sorts.'

'Because you fly, granddad says. You float on the roof.' He gestures towards my hands. His eyelids, his long lashes, I notice, droop like my brother's. 'And because you have one hand bare and one hand in a purple glove.'

I shrug. 'Does that make me only half magician?'

'Maybe.' He pauses. 'But I think it's 'cause you hide something.'

His words nick, little teeth, at my gloved hand.

'Why do you wear it?' he persists.

I shove both hands into my pockets. 'Scars.'

'You mean tattoos?'

Immediately, he pulls up his sleeve and displays his upper arm. The blood rises to my cheeks. I close my eyes before the brittle blue lines branded into his skin clarify into a number.

'Which …?'

He stares and waits for me to finish the question. My hand aches now. Tomek is making a rheumatism of my scars.

'Oświęcim,' he whispers.

Auschwitz, I translate. The town's name, in his tongue, is soft, but funereal. I wonder if it's his voice or my ears that sound sadness into each syllable. Once perhaps, those syllables, like brushes on cymbals, were simple and gentle. I try, for a moment, to imagine the pretty houses that might have stood next to the camps, the house that might have been his, the walls that might have been white or pink and the roofs tiled or slated or thatched.

'I'm sorry,' I whisper.

'Tomek!' His grandfather shouts again and proceeds to rattle, in Polish, what sound like instructions. Come down. Get away from the strange musician man. He can't understand. He's not one of us. Stay safe. Keep to ground.

Tomek sings a Polish lullaby back to his grandfather.

'I'd best start playing, eh?' I say. 'Give the bride and groom their first dance. And yourself! Don't you want a little dance too?'

Tomek nods. A swallow dips behind the boy, only an inch or two from his head, and then it rises again. The sky, as though a banner threaded to the bird's tail, turns a slate-blue. I feel thunder in the air.

'Tell me first.' The boy brushes his fingertips across my gloved hand. 'How did your hand scar?'

The boot crushes into my knuckles again. Glass bites into my palm.

'Just a stupid fight.'

'Tomek!'

'Go on now. Your granddad's missing you.' I lift my bow and shrill a note, hoping this gesture will be dismissal enough.

Tomek shakes his head. 'No. You don't understand. Granddad's not telling me to climb down.'

'What?'

'He's telling me to jump.'

I stare down at the small man looking up, his white hair slicked to his head like the sulphur on a matchstick. As I stare, I see he's smiling. He raises his hand and waves. I step back from the edge.

Tomek grins. 'He says he'll catch me.'

My heart thumps. 'From this height?'

'I'm only light.'

'Not when you jump!' I snap, wondering a moment if Tomek's fooling me, but grabbing at his shoulder nonetheless. My knuckles burn. 'You gather weight when you fall. Don't you know that?'

'No – I'll float, just like a swallow.'

His eyes are the brightest blue now, even his lashes. 'Are you both crazy?'

He laughs and wriggles his shoulder free from my grasp. My bow plucks a strangled note from the violin strings and falls. It bounces across the gutter, twirls upwards a moment and spins earthwards. The whirling ground below washes blue, suddenly underwater. Everything washes blue. The tiles. My violin. Tomek's face. We've drowned, without my noticing. And I see again the morning the SS first appeared on our streets and we woke underwater. The only things that knew how to gleam that day were Nazi badges and buckles. My heart compacted into blue slate – it took only a moment – beneath all those stamping feet.

Tomek's grandfather waves again. A spark of sunlight strikes him and his matchstick head burns. He stretches out his left arm and catches my tiny falling bow.

'See!' Tomek stamps his foot. 'It's easy.'

He shuffles to the roof's edge and raises both arms. He sees the sky as a sea too. I grab again at his neck.

'Don't! You'll be jam!'

His mouth curls. 'Jam?'

'Yes! Jam! Bright red jam. Fit for a giant's bread.'

'Giant bread?'

'You'll be troll meat.'

Tomek stops giggling and I wonder at my own words. His grandfather calls again.

'I jumped before!' he says, his eyes still a crazy gannet-blue. 'In the camp. From the top of a hut. And Grandpa caught me.'

I press both hands now around his chest. His small, fast heart thumps into my palms. I stare down at the gaping madman below, head still flickering. The camp must have driven the pair of them mad. Delusions became comfort. The old man thinks he can catch a boy falling from any height.

'Stop it!' I shout down.

The grandfather's cheeks blaze.

'Let him go!' he shouts back. His voice, in English, is deeper than in Polish.

Folk are gathering now around the old man. The black dog is there again, yapping. The landlord's mouth is agape. They're all staring upwards.

'He can't jump!' I yell. 'He'll break his neck.'

'I'll climb down –' Tomek leans into my arms, 'if you tell me.'

My hold loosens. 'Tell you what?'

'Where you're from.'

I clear my throat, as I always do, whenever I have to tell, in offices, in front of shining desks with inkbottles and poised nibs.

'Denmark.'

He stares. 'Near a camp?'

'No. We didn't have camps, not like—'

'Oświęcim?'

'They just came one day. And that was that,' I say. I imagine the entire crowd below listening to me, hushed. 'And we were occupied. Like Poland.'

'Occupied in one day? You didn't fight?'

Like we did, he wants to add.

My mouth dries. 'We tried.'

For six hours, Danish soldiers tried. The longest six hours ever lived. *Only six*, Tomek might answer. They were going to bomb Copenhagen, I want to explain – all those dark, roaring birds. We had no choice. No good choice. But we saved, quietly.

'They were too strong. And we were too few. But we never built camps. We refused the camps.'

I stare into his white face and I'm looking across the breakfast table at my brother's face that first lightless morning. The kitchen window had darkened into four slate tiles. Ralf tore a rag of bread and ripped it between the small teeth he usually kept hidden behind his lips.

'They'll want more soldiers,' he said. 'The Germans will want strong men, committed men.'

Moments later, the window was in shards as I punched and we fell and thrashed around the kitchen floor. Our parents stood in the doorway: my father watched in silence, while my mother watched my father and wept. Ralf grabbed a spear of glass. He cut first.

'It's all right. Other people fought for us all,' Tomek says, patting my hand.

I blink and wonder at his speaking of 'us'. He doesn't see my brother walking towards him, the felling slate-blue sky he carries with him, the long thorn of glass. Ralf stares at me again across the breakfast table. 'Strong, committed men,' he repeats. I close my eyes.

Tomek strokes my gloved wrist. The sky lightens behind my eyelids. 'It's all right,' he says.

I open my eyes and look into his pink face and I realise.

'You made up the story about jumping?'

Tomek laughs and I see the red back of his throat. He leans forwards as though he means to fly. And for a moment, I see him sail through the sky, a curling kite, while his grandfather below steers the string with his large, calloused hands. And I wish I were that man steering this flying boy. The next moment, Tomek sighs and leans back into my reaching hands.

He glances up at me and winks. 'It's all right. I'll use the ladder today.'

I look away again from Ralf's blue stare. I turn from my parents who stood by the door and watched. I tug at the glove on my itching hand, but I can't remove it. It's not all right, I want to say. I didn't stop Ralf.

'Will you be gone tomorrow?' he asks.

I nod.

He begins to descend the ladder. When his chin nuzzles the gutter, he smiles.

'It's true. I did jump,' he says. 'I flew. And you fly too.'

'What?'

'Yesterday. And the day before. Every time you play your violin. Far above the terrace you fly. And we follow.'

Tomek frowns. He whispers a word to himself. He clears his throat. 'Reverent.'

Alec Finlay

THE RIVER OF CONCEPTION

after Samuel Johnson, A Journey to the Western Isles of Scotland

Every meaningful journey needs a *Shirakwa*: a gateway through which travel and purpose align. Dr Johnson's was a nameless '*small stream*' near Loch Cluanie, whose '*green bank*' he set himself down upon, '*to take notes*', '*in the midst of savage solitude, with the mountains before me, and on either hand covered with heath*'. In his letters he confesses that he does not feel equal to the place, '*I wondered that I was not more affected, but the mind is not at all times equally ready to be put in motion*', but it was here, with many miles covered, that Dr Johnson tells us the idea for his book was born.

I. Loch Cluanie

'*He told us, he now recollected that he dreamt the night before, that he put his staff into a river, and chanced to let it go, and it was carried down the stream and lost.*'—James Boswell

I sat down for a time
   on a green bank
   with a small stream
      at my foot

I felt myself confined
   in the circumference
   of a narrow horizon
      of savage solitude

I shaped   my erratic back
   to the buffer
   of a boulder

let my thoughts range
over those last miles
of ling   treeless moss
   and sharp rush

the moor   punctuated
   by burnt roots

the wild mechanics
   of dividing mountains

that have kept on   rocking
   my short mount

it's grand to be motionless
grand   to have my eyes
   hindered

         to be released
from the infomatic
   spate

grand   to bend my mind
   to the flexanimous current
   of   whatever dark river
                        this is?

   which could be thought
      into a book   like
            the account kept
               by my loquacious
                  friend

     while the pool exchanges
brief eddies   for stillness
   my mind seems
      to have broken
         into   excursion

            as a *Journey*

II. Glen Aray

     This is night then   is it?

         this rim of light
            delayed   by shade

added to the dim
   I can discern
      the sullen din
      of another cataract

            pouring its roar
                              over

               the ceaseless
                  pitter-
         patter

      of this quotidian
      Scottish rain

I have come   bare
   into this far   weather

such barbarous   wetness

such cloying   peatmoss

such blasting winds

   blowing their proprie-
     torial noise
      all over this
        general bareness

aye, well may you ask
   of this *classic ground*

     where the place?
     upon the heath

well you may query
   this day's   hard journey

    far from the meridian
     light

    I am too, too   deep
     in the pine's
       twilit enchantment

      how much longer
      must I limn
      the waters

in this useless
        country
that has sunk   my spurs
and robbed me
of my good old
        oak staff?

here I am – ridiculous,
     on this ridiculous mount
     which drags my buckles
        in the mud and ruts –

but, you should know,
    I have numbered
    these streams!

fifty-five – in ten miles –

    and that there, falls
    as the *fifty-sixth*!

            believe me   counting
          has done nothing
              to quench
              their nonsense

soon the time will come
    to pause

to write the moment
out from the hills grasp

to converse at a distance
from stone and waste

matters vague form-
   less   foolishness

III. Inveraray Castle

tonight I will recollect
  all this noise   as
    rough music

    and give the nameless
    flushing rivulets
      names
        more fitting for maps

tonight   I will sit
  within the common-
    sense arc
    of a steady lamp

with leisure
for contemplation

I will diminish
the force's
   chaos with the dip
      of my pen

I will shape
a lexical sense
and soften summits   into cones
   fit for the frames
   of arithmetical windows

I will alphabetise   the rain
   into the singular line
   of my own ligature

   for only the civility
   of ordered letters
   can truly moderate
   the whirling dance
      of experience

willingly   I will
   trade in   all of these
      robust memories

   for a book that buds
         from the steady branches
         of my thoughts

This poem is a summary of a journey, Out of Books, *inspired by Boswell and Johnson's journey across the Highlands and Islands in 1773, made with Ken Cockburn in 2012.*

Cheryl Follon

INSOMNIA

I took my insomnia down the white hot heat of a two-mile strip of kebabists, ice-cream parlours, waffles, New Balance shoes and gypsy dancing. We got to spend the time together we usually didn't get. We had a waffle and cream and insomnia told me about its plans for the future, its dreams.

BLOOD

Blood's kept busy around the orange TVs, old suede two-seaters, backgammon boards and teacups at Peter's Market – everywhere, really. A little more effort required at the soft grey dust of the old films. Plenty of work at the hospital. There's not much time for anything else, really, but blood manages – squeezes in what it can.

BROGUES

A man from Boston got brogues going – after a first-class childhood spent with his feet up on his granny's great expensive cabinets and looking at the framed photos of the dead pets. The dead pet photos were all gone, and so was granny's house, but he relived the experience again and again by wrapping the closest he could get to those big cabinets around his feet and he got the brogues going.

Lesley Glaister

STROLL

From our friends' window
I saw you on the road
in your pale coat

a blob of white
black bobbing at your heels
our dog.

Only a shrinking mark
you were smaller than a bean
rounding a bend and

gone. I felt a chill
and during all the chatter
kept surreptitious watch till

you in pale coat
with bounding dog
came visible again

came smiling in
with absolutely no idea

how far you'd been.

Andrew Greig

INGRID, ANTHEA, LATE KANDINSKY

'Just as there are enough dead triangles, there are just as many dead horses, dead roosters, or dead guitars.'—Wassily Kandinsky

Every bright thing you look at long and hard enough
    sooner or later oozes black outline
that for a while heightens the colour within.
    As death seeps down from grandparents to parents,

to peer then friend then child,
    and the first body you once knew as flesh
within living flesh, goes up in smoke,
    and the next rots in the ground,

it gets so even the living are scarcely there,
    like passers-by in early photographs,
their own ghosts as they go on urgent business.
    The black outline thickens like a waistline.

I want to shed a few pounds of death,
    I think incoherently as my bus pass goes unchallenged,
and watch that baby guzzling its demise
    in the guise of a ring-pull dummy.

It seems I am thinking on that Kandinsky retrospective
    at the Tate, one summer in the Eighties, doubtless on
one of my below-the-radar trips to London,
    custodianed by Anthea or Ingrid von Essen

– both long dead, which is probably why
    I falter on ascription, scrawl *Dead woman friend*
as caption for this memory out-take
    where her hand demonstrates how Naturalism

begins its long slog towards Abstraction
       when Death enters the picture (Wassily's child
must not be mentioned, ever) in the second gallery.
       Sheep, clouds, Cossacks, a stoical cow

poised by a river, lances and church, all become
       ringed in black, insistently as a pissed-off child
who believes if he sulks hard enough, the world
       will have to give him a break, make an exception

so this time ice-cream comes with chocolate sauce,
       and no one has to die. It worked? You stopped?
Of course not! So you'll understand the phase
       when cow, river, Cossacks drop out, as though someone

had taken a paper-punch to canvas, leaving only
       black outline, bullet hole, the shape of that singular
absence. Focused on that,
       you cannot tell one dead friend from another,

their death has hollowed out your heart, leaving
       only the shape of their going.
'Abstraction is born not from geometry
       but seeing death everywhere – as of course it is.'

Ah yes, that must be Ingrid. I have installed
       her death's head face, near-white Finnish hair –
a sliver of glacier wrapped in black leather,
       blue glittering stare, that blink and you missed it smile

brief as winter sunlight in Helsinki, into this scene.
    (This before our foolish falling out, unresolved
before cancer punched her out of the picture
    leaving only black, ache, the shape of absence;

Anth must have stayed home that day, glass
    by clear glass becoming fuzzy then speechless
till one Xmas morning only a red outline
    lay stretched across the bed.)

If the dead were watching – I think not, but we
    do watch on their behalf, as though
their non-existent vanishing point
    props up the illusion 'Real Life' – they'd say

Get a grip, you lucky living bastard,
    and take my arm, as Ingrid did
– Were we? Did we ever? You must be joking –
    that fetid summer in the Eighties, and tug me

through the transition phase, that doomy passage
    of nothing but black outline and non-specific grey,
into the space where late Kandinsky blazes
    vast blues of the sky behind the sky

against which spindles, prawns, impossibly balancing
    spires, cylinders, moons green, vermillion, yellow
and, yes, black, small globes of black rolling
    down inclined planes of colour, black

as one more abstraction in a colour field:
    'The shape of the sound of Moscow's bells',
'Alternative music for mind and senses',
    'In love with things but not dependent on them' –

Pure ploy! Inexhaustible splendour
    of the presence of absent friends!
Lead me on, Ingrid, take me home, Anthea,
    lead me from this world of black outline

to the gallery where jokes and balances
    precisely poise in incandescent blue,
then re-enter the world that knows us
    brimming with itself, as Anthea gestures at the sky,

and Ingrid looks sideways at me, her transient smile
    drilled into my heart as we cross
Trafalgar Square, then on to whatever
    will become of me, and them, and us.

Brian Hamill

THE TOOTH

It is morning now, and only his head is poking out from the covers. The sound of the dripping tap, annoying him for the last few hours. Drip, drip, dripping. He has imagined it as two glasses being chinked together, an old blacksmith with a steady hammer, and other things. Ah but fuck this. He throws the quilt off and gets up.

He's in the shower when it breaks. The whole thing doesn't fall out but part of it snaps somehow, when clenching the top and bottom rows together. The impact makes his head shudder, and the piece is down his throat before he knows it. He boaks. Spit and red drop from his lips onto the surface of the bath. He moans though there's no pain, puts his finger softly in the side of the mouth. There's around half left, the split going right down the middle and leaving a jaggy thing, a shard, sharp to the touch. When he takes the fingertip back out it's covered in warm black blood.

Waiting, staring at the blackness of it.

The bathroom mirror is now all condensation and the air's thick with steam, so he wraps a towel round and goes to the bedroom. Sits at the dresser and pulls his cheek out using his thumb, but more dark fluids escape and hit the carpet. He swears and pulls the towel off to scrub before it stains. The fucking alarm clock blaring again, to let him know he should be leaving the house. Late again. The boss will be angry. He jogs back to the bathroom, rubs the mirror with the towel and leaves brownish streaks of saliva across. Soon as the toothbrush passes his front teeth he gags and leans over the sink, deep breaths. No vomit comes. His eyes full of water.

In the bedroom he tries to rush the clothes on, overbalances while struggling with the bastard second sock. The wardrobe breaks his fall. It shakes. He feels a new stream of air flowing round his mouth whenever there's a breath in. Coldness coming from the side and drying his tongue, like when a draught gets in from the window and blows the household things about. When dressed, he packs the inside of his cheek with tissues.

Already late, so takes time for his morning coffee anyway. The first sip runs into the wound, and for a horrible moment he feels it's slipped down into somewhere it should never be; the interior of the jaw, the frame of his skull, the muscle and bone. The remaining liquid is spat into the kitchen bin. Had the taste of blood. He touches along his jawbone, but doesn't know what he's feeling for and stops. The tissue's now wet and heavy, a soaking ball squeezed against the lower teeth. He pulls it out, flakes into pieces in his hand. The smell is so strong it has to be stuffed down the side of the bin, buried as far as possible. The cuff of his shirt gets covered in curry sauce from the last night's takeaway. Too late to change. He is retching.

*

The bus to work is busy. His face is to the floor. No soreness, but it's oozing on to his tongue. He uses more and more tissues, turning to the window and pretending to blow the nose. It isn't clear if he's imagining it, but there's a new feeling, a sensation, inside. The broken piece, moving around his stomach. Hard like metal, the way you'd feel a knife if it was slipped in among the pillows at night, a coldness somewhere in the layers. His throat and chest start to ache, as if the piece, this fragment, the broken-off, has scraped its way down through the body. Had this happened to anybody before? Internal injuries due to swallowed tooth. Bit of tooth. Off tooth. The nurses in the casualty will have seen some cases.

He looks out the window. The streets packed, a flow of people speeding to work, rushing so they don't get into trouble. Trouble. He's been warned about timekeeping, his record of punctuality, and the tooth won't be considered a good excuse, not by his boss. Coming from somebody else, perhaps. Not him.

A raised voice coming from the front and he looks up. Somebody leaning into the driver's booth and shouting. An older lady, shaking her head and pointing to the road outside. He notices a woman on the other side, few rows down. She's the only person turning to face back up the bus as people look forward at the argument. She catches his eye and smiles. All her teeth. Not shining white, but they are straight and strong. Greying, grainy squares all locked in together, perfect, not one row slotted in front of the other like is often seen.

He returns to staring at the street. Smiling back would show blood, or the wound.

The bus clatters along the road leading to his building. It's one of the main streets the buses use, stops all the way down one side. The many years of the double-deckers pulling in, sitting, driving off, has worn big holes in the tarmac. Now everything rattles noisily as it goes, tyres banging down then up with the potholes. He really thinks he can feel the broken-off being thrown around inside him, every bump that shakes him in his seat then swirls the contents of his stomach. It must be stabbing the sides, hurting him. His hands move to his belly. The shard could pierce something. Would, probably. Something vital. It could rip right through the lining, then what? Dead. Stomach acid pouring round organs, burning them up, things sizzling and dissolving. He wipes his face with his hand. The flesh, not willing.

Relief when the bus arrives outside the office, and he can get away from the people and into fresh air for a second. In the foyer he nods to Terry the guard and keeps walking before conversation can start. The reception desk standing empty. He hits the button for the lift and moves his tongue about. The broken one just to the left of the front set, maybe the gap and the craggy remain will be seen if he laughs or gets talking. Looking like a dog. Or an old man. A tramp. A few people say good morning, but he's going too fast to stop and keeps the smile tight, short and tight.

He turns his seat to point into the corner. The computer is warming up when his friend Douglas comes up behind. Douglas is just over for a natter before the big meeting. He natters about wee Rochelle from the sixth floor. Douglas asks if he'd do wee Rochelle and he nods. He keeps his head tilted, taking glances at Douglas and nodding now and then. Silence. Douglas finishes his cuppa then wanders away. The online calendar pings and shows a reminder that it's meeting time. He considers sending Douglas a quick email.

The meeting is long and dull. He's too junior to have to speak. He slides down in the chair and stretches his legs. The wound has stopped bleeding, as long as he doesn't touch it with the tongue. He breathes in and out his nose. The boss is pointing at the ceiling and everybody is laughing. Everybody laughing at the funny joke. They go back to talking, and he realises that the tooth still there, the left-behind, will need to come out. His eyes close. The air conditioning is rippling the top page of his notepad. The last time he had a tooth out he was still at school. A woman dentist. She pulled and pulled at the rotted molar, couldn't budge. She yanked it so hard his head was coming off the chair and his throat was gasping for air. The nurse went next door and got the man dentist. He had a thing over his mouth, but winked his eye and patted the patient's shoulder. He put his leg up on the chair, pressed down on the forehead with one hand, took the plier things in the other. The memory is always fresh, the feeling of the man dentist's knuckles and hands and arms, brown curled hairs rubbing against his lips and his face. There was a crunch when the tooth was dragged out of the gum, then all he could see was the light above. He lay back and had all the blood and the mess sucked out by the nurse and the grey tube. The nurse shoved it in and the tip of the tube could be felt knocking against the back of the throat, and the windpipe, prodding, prodding into the tissues, but you were tired, too tired, and so you just lay, you lay waiting.

Seats being pushed out, and people are standing up. The meeting is finished. He goes to his desk and faces the screen. Some time later Linzi appears in the booth with a card to sign. He tries to smile and make some right noises, but Linzi asks what he's being a weirdo bastard for then walks away, her high heels clicking along the corridor. Click, click, click, click. Regular, like the morning's tap that dripped.

*

He's in the bathroom waiting for the guy in the other cubicle to leave. He won't afford a dentist. Not at the moment, his situation. They'd either pull out what's left and fit a full new tooth, or build something on to the remaining bit. Both would be expensive. His friend who died had been a dentist so he knows what they charge.

The piece of tooth is still inside his body, floating somewhere, sharp as a razor blade. If it would pass through him when he has a shit. It must. And will do damage on the way. He notices his foot tapping against the floor tiles. The other guy washes his hands and the door bangs shut. He comes out and smiles into the mirror. It can be seen. Normal teeth on the top, normal teeth on the bottom all the way along, then a slice of red gum, the shadow of a tooth further in. An animal's face. He spits in the sink. The mixture is red, black and clear, different globules hanging together loosely. It slides downwards in the basin and he starts being sick.

The boss has sent him an email, saying to get back to the meeting room at his earliest convenience. He replies, saying he must go home. As soon as the message is sent, he heads for the lift. There's tension building in the tooth, it's throbbing through his head and he needs it out, now. The bit should not be there; it is no longer a tooth. The lift door opens and Terry is there, smiling, asking questions about the game last night. Terry shouts after him, wanting to know what's wrong, but he doesn't look back. Another person calls his name from reception, probably Susie. Can't fucking talk. The door swings behind and the sunlight's warm on his skin.

His mouth is shut tight all the way home. The pain is there now, the walls of his stomach are sore. The piece is jabbing into them, scratching on surfaces. People in the street either look at him and stare, or they don't notice him at all. Nobody cares what goes on inside other folk. Walk on. It's a hot day and there's sweat on his face, on his upper lip and trickling into the corners of the mouth. He stops the moaning noise he's making before people hear.

His cousin is a pharmacist, she could get some anaesthetic. If it wouldn't be too much trouble. If his face was numbed right, he could get somebody to rip it out. It doesn't take a dentist to get a grip on something and pull. He cuts up a side street in the shadow, away from the main road, remembering a story his old girlfriend told him about a friend from work. The woman got a tooth took out when she was on holiday, somewhere in South America, and the wound wouldn't clot. Her jawbone was left exposed, the gum was all cut up, and she got an infection. When in the hospital. A disease in her face. He needed somebody who knew the right way to pull a tooth. A vet would know. Maybe a butcher. They'd need paid.

*

The house is quiet. He goes straight to the bedroom and under the covers. He doesn't want to look like this. Smashed fucking wonky rotten teeth. Disgusting bloody cut gums. He hooks his finger in and pulls at the tooth. He can't move it, and the feeling. Runs round all the bones in his head and makes him scream. Even behind his eyes throbs with the pain, a pulse which is moving the eyeballs.

An hour later he gets up again, and he's in the bathroom when the front door gets chapped. He asks who it is. It's Julie, his neighbour. She shouts through the door that Douglas sent her a message. Douglas said he was acting strange at work, and then disappeared from his desk. Douglas has spoke to the boss and thinks he should get back to work, now. Good old Douglas. Thanks, Douglas. Tell Douglas thanks. Julie thinks he should open the door so she can see him. But fuck off, Julie. A nosey neighbour wanting to see the animal face. Wolfman. He has always fancied Julie, and it's not easy to poke the letter box open and shout at her to go the fuck away and fuck off, fuck off, Julie, trying to see in, but not able to as he stands back from the door and cannot be seen.

Julie walks slowly back to her place. She sits on the front step. Has a cigarette, then another. The sun beats down. Her phone buzzes again. She goes back to his house but doesn't chap on the door. From the path that runs round his house she can see in the front window. She watches. He is making different smiles at himself in the glass. Then shaking his head, shouting, crying, trying to do another smile. He shouts and bashes his hand off the frame of the mirror. It jolts around on its hook, and she sees herself in it. A quick flash of her face, staring in the window. They both watch it come back to a standstill.

Lesley Harrison

SELF PORTRAIT
Margaret Tait, Orkney film-maker 1918–1999

a house and a garden
a garden of doors
a door to a room
a room full of islands

a calm within walls
a wall with a mirror
a mirror and eye
an eye full of silver

a pram and an anchor
a boat in a field
a field full of sunlight
the sun on the pavement

a line in a road
a road full of wind
a wind without colour
the colour of water

Sylvia Hays

TISSUE

It has happened once more, that freshly opening another W. G. Sebald essay – 'Le promeneur solitaire' / 'A remembrance of Robert Walser' – has brought to life a memory, this time of an event that took place in 1975. I utterly forgot it soon after; was it even an event? What constitutes an event? Every moment, conscious or unconscious, sleeping or awake? A lifetime?

Though I have long been interested in German literature I had never heard of Robert Walser. Sebald begins: 'The traces Robert Walser left on his path through life were so faint as to have almost been effaced altogether ... Nowhere was he able to settle, never did he acquire the least thing by way of possessions.' The memory hadn't emerged quite yet; it was waylaid by my musing at length about possessions, about the wish that I once had to have more, and about a simultaneous, quieter subplot about the desire to have none; too, about the implications of each desire for the sort of existence that would be lived in consequence; and, inevitably, about wanting to encompass the two opposites.

Only with Sebald's mention of 'the writer's millions of illegible ciphers' did the nearly obliterated memory begin to take visible form. I was spending 1975 in Boston, though I had no reason of my own, that is, no reason as a painter, to be there. I still had an enormous and very ugly Dodge station wagon, bought a couple of years before from someone in the English Department of the institution from which I had recently resigned. The vehicle was cheap, and it was large enough to carry my paintings as long as they measured not much more than six feet by about four. I loaded a group of recent paintings into the Dodge and drove them down to New York, intending to introduce myself and my work to some of the galleries.

Somehow I fell into conversation with a young man who seemed to be making similar rounds, though he had no work with him that I could see. The gallery was somewhere in downtown Manhattan – it might have been in SoHo – so called for the area south of Houston Street. It was on an upper floor of a tall building that contained a variety of other firms. We shared the elevator up. Damian – yes, his name comes back to me – asked, 'What do you smell?' I breathed deeply and said, 'Hot dogs.' 'IFF operates in the building,' he said. To my blank look he explained, 'International Flavors and Fragrances.' I didn't know of them, but the idea amused me that they could imitate almost anything that presented itself to two of our senses, that they were constantly formulating more tastes and smells as diligently as Niebelungs enslaved to Alberich, hammering for gold. There would be commercial applications for all this research, persuading people to want more, buy more, but it didn't occur to me then, as the elevator took us upwards, that I probably had already been manipulated by IFF, if only to buy some freshly baked bread.

The gallery won't quite come into focus; it retains a dreamlike vagueness out of which emerge an entrance door, a reception desk off to the right, and a large open space emanating a vapour the colour of cream thickening to a darkish yellow around the edges. I don't know what had made me choose to visit it; Damian, I had the impression, had been there before. That visit produced nothing; nothing, I imagine, for either of us, though it had taken place amiably enough. The elevator was taking us down when Damian asked, 'What do you smell now?' 'Roses.' We must have stood outdoors for a little while talking about our work. He seemed interested in mine; of his, he said, 'I'll send you some.' So we exchanged addresses and I, disbelieving him, soon forgot about the long thin man who was so colourless as to approach transparency, whose colourless lank hair stirred with the dust that eddied or gusted off the city streets.

I am questioning my memory as if I expected it to respond to me with truth: verifiable, objective, unassailable. I wonder whether I misremember the name of IFF, whether it ever existed; whether likening its researchers to dwarves slaving for Alberich in *Das Rheingold* was a simile stretched too far, though it cropped up through some workings, invisible to me, of spontaneous unreason. So I have recourse to the internet, find the firm, read its official website and its Wikipedia entry. International Flavors and Fragrances has an interesting history. It was formed in 1958 from a merger between two companies, one of which, van Amerigen & Co., was located at 13 Gold Street, Manhattan. By 2000 IFF had made an acquisition that made it the largest firm of its kind in the world. But there were lawsuits, one against its subsidiary.

There were 'cases of bronchiolitis obliterans allegedly resulting from an exposure to diacetyl in butter flavorings by workers at the Glister-Mary Lee popcorn plant in Jasper, Missouri', in other words, 'Popcorn Lung'. Wikipedia also tells us that the Chairman and CEO is Doug D. Tough. From IFF's own website I learn that its Global Headquarters is at 521 West 57th Street, New York, that 'IFF is committed to being a good global citizen' and that its share price is just over $100 per share. No mention of 'Popcorn Lung'; the search results suggest 'portion lunch'.

Of course there can be no causal connection between today's search and my next move, in 1975, to visit another gallery located on West 57th Street, not unless it is possible for time to run backwards. The determination of that I must leave to physicists and philosophers, whereupon I've been distracted by another search, this time for works by my ex-husband, who died in 1986. I find a bibliography of his papers on the philosophy of mind, among which is 'Events and Time's Flow', published in *Mind* in 1987. I am intrigued by the title but cannot access the paper. It is as if he were arguing his case, or keeping silent, from the grave.

The 57th Street gallery was in a neighbourhood of steel, plate glass, marble and improbably thick pale carpets. The director was surprisingly approachable. My footsteps were muffled as I followed him to his office. Would my paintings feel at home here, I wondered. The director pronounced them beautiful, powerful even, and didn't confuse the meticulous realism that I was engaged in at the time with photorealism, from which I stood at a painterly and metaphysical distance. Despite a sympathetic response the result was the same here: nothing more.

From uptown I launched the Dodge downtown, fitting my driving technique to the speeding river of yellow cabs. I was back in SoHo, in an area still rough and ready, still with industrial lofts not all converted to the use of big-name artists and others who required grand areas of living space but spurned Park Avenue. The name of this gallery would be hard to forget: OK Harris, Works of Art. The name was fictitious and suggested the persona of some tough riverboat gambler, according to its owner Ivan Karp. Ivan himself was such a blatant character that he would dominate any environment he might have been in; the riverboat gambler as alter ego made sense. I expected him to detest my work, since he was occupied with promoting photorealism, but he asked to keep one of my paintings for a matter of months, perhaps because he misunderstood its intent.

Uptown again, another painting was taken in by a large gallery on Madison Avenue where it consorted with slick advertising agencies. It was hung near a plate-glass window where it might be seen from the street by ad men on their way to work, or by shoppers who had strayed over from Fifth Avenue. If the painting had eyes to see – can I be sure it did not? – it might have been puzzled by its audience, and they by it. One last errand took me down into the Bowery, at that time in steep decline from its nineteenth-century grandeur. Flophouses lined the streets; men begging were at every corner. I had been warned to keep the car doors locked and the windows rolled up. I had to stop at a red light. While I was pinned in place waiting for the light to change a man came over to the car. He pulled from his pocket a thin, dirty piece of something that might have been a handkerchief. He climbed on to the hood and started to wipe the fragment across the dry, dusty windshield with one hand while holding out his palm with the other. I shook my head without meeting his eyes. Mine were focused on the red light. The light turned green; traffic was beginning to move. I let the car inch forward as slowly and gently as possible so that the man, who was very drunk, could detach himself without getting hurt. I drove off feeling like a complete shit; feeling, too, the rebuke of the thick carpets that still seemed to tingle under my feet.

Back in Boston, I unloaded the paintings that remained, recovered from my journey and settled down to work in the room I was using as a studio. It was one of those happy periods when ideas come unforced and unbidden, and in such numbers that only a few of them can take physical form. The rest are never quite discarded, but stored away in some half-conscious underworld where they continue to murmur: why haven't you chosen us? why not let us out? The next painting so absorbed me that the New York excursion was out of mind until the day a brown envelope arrived in the post. The spidery tortured handwriting told me that it must be something from Damian. As I extracted some tightly folded tissue paper from the envelope it unbent in slow arthritic stages. The thin white paper had been knifed and scissored into attenuated forms that, even when I raised my arm over my head, dangled to the floor. The same spidery handwriting covered the complicated shapes.

What did it say? I could never quite decipher it. There were sequences of letters that almost became words, but never did a string of them make any kind of sense. This was not a work of beauty (though I don't require of art that it be beautiful); it was not poetry. It gave me an inward shudder. Every week or two another such envelope arrived, with a similar tissue-and-ink artefact that had required long hours of labour. The accumulated body of work underscored the sense I had had when I met Damian, that some variety of madness inhabited him. I never replied to any of these offerings and eventually they ceased. I bundled up all the paper one day and put it out with the trash. It niggled at me that I had so firmly put aside that faint brush with presumed madness, and now that I have remembered it, prompted by Sebald's essay, I wonder whether I had failed, out of timidity or cowardice, to recognise something of value, however odd. Of Robert Walser's intricate texts, Sebald sees 'that their peculiar preoccupation with form ... or the way that their length is determined by the exact dimensions of the space available on a scrap of paper, exhibit certain characteristics of pathological writing: an encephalogram, as it were'; yet he does not accept them as evidence of a psychotic state. Eventually Walser did become a broken man, and finished his days in an asylum, 'scrubbing vegetables in the kitchen, sorting scraps of tinfoil or ... just standing stiffly in a corner.' In coming to that end he was in company with Hölderlin, with Kleist, with Schumann and others who make up a ghostly, solitary multitude.

Months later I returned to New York to collect my paintings. The one on Madison Avenue hadn't sold; at OK Harris it was difficult to catch Ivan Karp in flight across the gallery with his retinue to ask about my other painting. He stood still long enough to shout 'That painting is famous! I've put it into exhibitions all over New York! Now you can take it away.' I wanted to ask him which exhibitions, where, what company my work had kept; and there might have been lines to add to my CV, but he took wing again.

Jules Jack

IN DUNDEE

In Dundee, he was sent off on a boat, as his gambling debts were an embarrassment to his family, who made the ships' harpoons to kill the whales.

The main creditor said, 'If you bring me a beautiful, exotic parrot, a boy parrot, then I will forget your debts, the parrot will sit in my parlour and he will sit on the iron gate to my grand house in the Perth Road during the summer … His wings will be clipped and a chain attached and all the children will remember this parrot and tell their children and their children's children.'

So he found the parrot from a man who sold jewels: the parrot was a baby in an ornate gold and sea-pearl cage, and he fed him delicious dried fruit and nuts; he bought a sapphire ring from the same man for the girl who drank in the Seagate Bar. He didn't know if she loved him but she loved to drink rum and peppermint.

And he bought sweet spicy oils for his mother, who loved him the most of all her children, as he was red-haired and generous, the kindest with the most flaws and had been conceived in great rapture but not with her husband.

On the rough sea journey back home, the ship hit a great storm: the parrot took great fright and plucked and lost his feathers in three days and three nights of rumbustious storm. They felt sure to die but emerged, as if baptised, into the still, strange, huge calm.

So when they arrived in Dundee, the beautiful orange and green parrot was worse than a scraggy chicken in a Hilltown butchers but the gambling debt was honoured when the parrot grew handsome, sage and gallus.

And what of the girl in the Seagate Bar, well she took the sapphire and sold it for drink and the following spring she gave birth to a red-headed baby who his mother took in. His mother rubbed the baby's legs, arms and tummy with the sweet-scented oil, and wheeled the baby proudly in his high pram on sunny days, to visit the beautiful orange and green parrot on the Perth Road.

*

Grandpa and I walked most days down to the old ferry slipway, in the village of Seaport, and looked across the haar-held Tay to Dundee. He thought it important that he walked every day as his sea-captain grandfather, he of the gambling debts, had ended up so fat that when he died in his bath, it took his four unmarried daughters to lift him out. Grandpa couldn't bear to foresee such humiliation.

'He must have been like the Tay Whale in that bloody bath, toots,' he would say.

This was 1981, the year of Bobby Sands, who I was half in love with, and the royal wedding; I was fourteen.

Grandpa wished that the ferry still ran; you could see the faded sign for ice cream on the walls, still can, and he remembered the elephants, horses and camels of the circus queuing up nobly, to sail to Dundee. He told me that the ferry had closed at times of plague and that the ferry had often been used to get rid of rogues from Dundee, Fife was their hope and their salvation … Grandpa's great-uncle Davey had worked on the ferry. Grandpa said that, having suffered a bad blow in the boxing booths, Davey had taken to drink and cared not for his wife or his life. His wife eventually left for Shetland with a sober whaler who was passing through. The Shetlander carried a sealskin purse with more money than he could spend, and he carried away Davey's wife.

It was on the ferry slipway that we first met the Chinaman. It was the year that he opened the Yangtze River in Dundee.

Jo Chung bought a grand smugglers' house in Seaport with the money flowing in from the Yangtze. It hung down on three floors to the Tay and there was a tunnel to the pebbled beach. When he wasn't at the Stakis casino in Dundee, he was in this house, at his table with the inlaid mother-of-pearl, precious stones and abalone, formed in the shape of a leaping tiger, playing mah jongg. The house was built in the Italianate style, like no other house in the village. They were all grey, carved-up jute barons' houses, some still haunted by the ancient, unmarried daughters still surrounded by their Edwardian entrapments; Grandpa's neighbours, the Misses Crawford, sat in the summer on hooded deckchairs behind their laburnum tree. Just along the braes from Jo, they woke to the same sight of the often angry Tay, or the Tay glistering blue, dipping the treacherous sand banks.

It was in Jo's curious and half-dead house, where all the windows faced north, still with the carriageway built by the Presbyterian minister, where I could feel the people from the past around me, that I was to hear the stories of his grandfather, the Chinese Illusionist. He had travelled, as part of his tour of Scotland, to the Whitehall Theatre in Dundee. The brittle, yellow newspaper clipping told us his magic had been 'as fascinating and quaint' as it was 'mystifying and marvellous'.

He read this to me from an old *Evening Times* review of his grandfather which he kept in a scratchily drawn Chinese pot. His grandfather's evening of entertainment (performed twice nightly due to popular demand) had included 'a gracious assistant, Miss Su Seen; a large staff of Chinese acrobats and dwarves; plate spinners and knife throwers with a human target; and the evening was finished with a suffragette sketch to the tune of "Excelsior".

We got drunk on rice wine and he told me of Chinese horoscopes and of arriving in Dundee where a terrible haar hung over the city for three days. He told me that it was a very auspicious year for marriage and he must marry soon.

I told him of the parrot and the gambling debts and my sea-captain great-great-grandfather and his famous ship's cat, Moses.

Andy Jackson

THE NAMING OF HURRICANES

Sometimes in summertime a hangdog
weather man stands in front of shots

panning over Caribbean villas mangled
into matchwood, corpses of beached yachts,

palms ripped from sand. A time-lapsed arc
maps the march of this year's cyclone,

wheeling to make its landfall, jerk
the world around it. Last year's was *Joan*,

a hurricane with personality – in yer face,
busy, our eyes drawn to her in photographs

as she breezed in and out, visible from space,
leaving nothing standing in her path.

I wonder who compiles the list of names;
whose mother, daughter, lover, wife

brings to mind such desolation. The Janes
and Brendas all suggest ordinary life

might yet return once the summer storm
has blown itself into a half-remembered breeze.

Here, so far from paradise, the house is warm,
but colder winds are forecast from the east,

and suddenly the sky is full of clouds. A chill
simmers round my feet, and I think it's best

we do not name this storm. Already it has filled
the room, blown your final letter off my desk.

Vicki Jarrett

THE MUTABLE LIGHT

Driving north, flicking through the radio stations, searching for anything without sleigh bells. I give up, choose silence. Not quite total silence, there's the stoic thrum of the engine and the whisper of finely milled slush under the wheels. Useful, purposeful sounds. Sounds of travelling, of distance gained. The surrounding fields are sealed in snow and the temperature is so low the casing has set to a fierce glitter. I try to keep my eyes on the road but my gaze is drawn towards the moon. She is slung fat and low in the sky, just one night past full.

Something thuds against the windscreen, then another and another, too fast for me to see. I peer into the funnel of light my headlights push into the darkness. Moths. Surely not at this time of year. But there they are. Lots of them. Winged confetti burling and straining between me and the moon. I grip the steering wheel as a shudder travels from my shoulders down the length of my arms to my hands.

Moths bother me in a way that makes my tongue curl back in my mouth. Butterflies too, despite being prettier to look at. Alien. The way they change so completely. It's as though they're mocking us by making it look easy. Ignoring the rules and principles of steady growth towards maturity by choosing instead a sudden and dramatic transformation into something entirely other. If a rabbit was to disappear into its burrow one winter and emerge in the spring re-engineered as a rhinoceros, for example, people would be alarmed. But Lepidoptera seem to get away with behaving this way and no one seems particularly fussed. Lepidoptera. Yes, I know the proper zoological name. I know more about the furry little bastards than I ever wanted to in a million years. This past month they've colonised my thoughts more than enough and I don't welcome this added intrusion.

*

I'd taken far longer than usual getting the images sized up for repro. Normally I'd have worked through a stack like that in no more than an hour, making notes on resizing and cropping for downstairs, marking up the galley proofs with insertion points, but I'd put off dealing with these pictures for a week since I first opened the Professor's parcel and flipped through the contents.

I didn't even like to touch the paper, the flimsy, clinging, faintly greasy sheets upon which the meticulous drawings were etched. There was too much detail, each veined wing beat at my defences, each probing proboscis reached out to lick at my eyeballs. The fat furry bodies twitching and curling on the page made my stomach contract. And the flowers these mutants crouched upon, petals flopping open, exposing glistening mounds of pollen perched upon turgid stamen. I wiped the sweat from my face, got up from my desk and opened the meagre fanlight of the only window in my office. By balancing on the pipe running under the radiator and using the bars on the window to pull myself up, I could taste the air from outside, illicit and cool. The surrounding rooftops formed a landscape of glass and red brick, strung together with cable and pipework that stretched as far as my limited viewpoint allowed. I closed my eyes and strained a little closer to the breeze and drew it into my lungs, to remind myself another world existed out there.

It's been three years since I migrated south for work, to a place somehow known as The North. The ghost of myself is always passing me on this road, driving in the opposite direction, full of optimism for a new start, a new life. Fresh. That's what they said at my first proper business lunch. 'This is Catriona. Fresh from Scotland!' Like I was a mature cheddar or a nice bit of smoked salmon, shipped down in a wooden crate overnight. They laughed and made jokes about unwrapping me. I smiled and looked down at the table. Wearing my new suit, with the green silk-looking blouse, tights and heels, hair tamed back into a twist, I had already recast myself in the shape of someone who didn't use the sort of language that battered for release behind my clenched teeth. I've got used to it. It's how things are and you adapt to fit in. You have to, or the predators will pick you off.

*

Another moth takes a spiralling kamikaze dive along my tunnel of light and headbutts the windscreen. It makes a loud dunt but leaves only a faint shimmery smear on the glass to show for its sacrifice. I put the windscreen wipers on rapid and pump screenwash until the car fills with a bitter lemony scent and all trace is gone.

Why couldn't the Professor just use photographs of the repulsive things instead of those psychotically precise drawings? I asked him when he came in to check on my progress.

'Well, I do photograph them, of course,' he smiled, 'it is after all unlikely that a subject would remain in position long enough for one to execute even a rudimentary sketch.' Stiff brown hair poked from between the unfastened buttons at the neck of his shirt and from under his cuffs. I tried not to imagine the segmenting of his abdomen under the muddy green knit of his tanktop.

'It's easy to press a button and capture a single moment but one misses so much. Photography renders the specimens … forgettable. To draw them, slowly and carefully by hand, teaches one so much more, about the body parts, yes, their textures and proportions, the way they fit together, but also about the personality of the specimen, its bearing. It's all in the process, the metamorphosis between photographic image and fully realised drawing. Think of Leonardo da Vinci with his exquisite renderings of human anatomy and early surgery. These were not only teaching tools, but learning tools, portals and routes to understanding. Do you see?'

'Yes,' I nodded. 'That's … well, that certainly explains it.' I laughed and shuffled the papers in front of me, hoping to draw a line under the conversation. Those beasts touched a part of me that didn't want to learn or understand. They left me yearning not for the light of knowledge, but for the blissful darkness of ignorance.

The Professor reached out and pinned a fluttering sheet under his extended finger.

'Ah, our old friend *Biston betularia*, the peppered moth.' He tilted his head and sighed. 'Our dauntless champion in the war against chaos.'

'I'm sorry?'

On the paper, two moths of the same size and shape, displaying the same *bearing*, as the Professor would put it, were drawn angled towards each other as though deep in conversation. Both had thick fur mantles and swooping feather-like antennae. But where the wings and body of one were white with a tasteful speckling of black, the other was dark as coal dust.

'Adaptation in action. This brave fellow is the most plainly observable and documented example of adaptive evolution. Of course, there are those, there always will be, who argue against it, but in rational circles, the evidence provided by the peppered moth is incontrovertible.'

I cleared my throat and swallowed. The moths seemed to incline closer together, broad-shouldered in their furs and feathers like aristocrats conferring on matters of consequence, excluding me from their conversation. It's only a drawing, I told myself, a drawing of insects, get a grip.

'To start with, this was the most common form. Morpha *typica*.' The Professor's bony finger traced around the lace-like wings of the pale moth. 'Its colouring provided camouflage as it slept during the day. But when the industrial revolution suffocated the lichens and blackened the trees, that light colour made them all too visible to the birds that lunched on them. The entire species may even have become extinct if it hadn't been for a few individuals that carried a specific genetic mutation resulting in much darker pigmentation.' The Professor drew an invisible lasso around the second moth. 'Morpha *carbonaria* thrived.'

I stared at the black moth. It looked smaller, denser than its lighter companion, although I knew they had exactly the same dimensions. I'd measured the drawings myself. The body, legs and antennae were all dark as pitch, the wings a semi-translucent, veined charcoal that seemed to reflect, even on paper, the frosty sheen of moonlight.

'But not any more! Now we have pollution control and nature is recovering. The lichens have regrown, the trees are once again white-barked. *Typica* has returned to dominance and *carbonaria* becomes rarer each year. This is what makes the peppered moth a perfect demonstration of natural selection. They adapt and survive.'

'Not all of them,' I said, caught out by the sudden emotion in my voice. 'I mean,' I continued, straining for a more measured tone, 'the ones that get eaten during these changes, because they don't fit in. They don't survive, do they?'

The Professor raised his bushy eyebrows and smiled slightly. 'No, dear, plainly not. But it's the survival of the species that matters.'

'Yes, I see that. I'm ... I'm sorry, I find them, moths in general I mean, not only these ...' I trailed off, embarrassed.

'No, no. Please, continue. How do you find them? Tell me.' The Professor leaned eagerly towards me.

'You'll think this is silly but … There's something *alien* about them, don't you think?'

The Professor's eyes lit up at once and he clapped his hands together, startling me. 'Yes! You're absolutely right, of course. That's exactly what drew me to Lepidoptera in the first place.'

Now I'd given him the opportunity, he went on at length, explaining the process of metamorphosis, talking about the discs of potential cells that exist in caterpillars or larvae and how, during the pupae stage, they develop into legs or wings or antennae. These cells somehow know what it is they're supposed to be and when to become it. The discs could also be moved. They'd done it to fruit flies.

'Dear God, is there anything that hasn't been done to fruit flies?' The Professor laughed, pleased with his joke.

He told me this research had shown that the leg cells would still grow as legs even if you put them where the eyes should be. I felt clammy and sick but the Professor seemed excited. He bristled and twitched as he spoke.

As he carried on talking, the failing sunlight reflected on his glasses, making it impossible to see his eyes. They were only blank discs. I blinked and tried not to see a pair of small human legs growing from his eye sockets. Limp dough-like skin sprouting dark hair, the toes pointed out as the tiny limbs flexed and contracted, blindly questioning, somehow aware that something monstrous had occurred and they were not where they should be.

*

So many times I've travelled this road, drawn back and forth between states of being, unable to decide on which end is the beginning and which end the end. The countryside glides by, perfectly mysterious under its binding of snow. How can the earth know what it should do when the snow finally melts?

How can it be that, despite the vast constellations of cells within my human body, all that potential, I still don't know where I belong or what I should be?

I've not seen another car for miles. Still the moths multiply, bliz-zarding now, the noise of them drumming on the windscreen like the impatient fingers of a hundred strange hands. I can barely make out the road ahead but know it so well I could navigate it blind. I switch off my headlights and, almost immediately, the noise stops. For a weightless moment the car is suspended in utter blackness, before the moon takes over. A huge pale disc.

Brian Johnstone

THE LAST TRAIN FROM ST FORT

Tickets for Dundee had been collected from passengers on the train before crossing the bridge. A photograph shows the tickets [of] some who lost their lives that night.

The Library of Nineteenth-Century Photography
– see the image at **bit.ly/st-fort**

They have the stubs, some fifty-six of these,
each punched, a blank triangle nicked
from every ticket's edge,

arranged into this neat display, framed up
and photographed, a wreath of non-arrival
commemorating those

they dredged out of the Firth, bedraggled
in their city clothes, or navvy's gear,
sandbanks seeping from the seams,

and carted lifeless through the streets
they would have stepped on to that night
but for the force and angle of the wind,

and workmanship so bad it might have been
deliberate neglect; or some sick joke,
like that the men made later

from his name, damned Bouch: the bodger
who had flung them from the edge
of certainty; dashed Victorian assurance

that their Bradshaw was reliable,
the engineering sound; nothing could delay
the locomotive, not yet renamed the *Diver*

as it would later be, hauled out of the deep,
uncoupled from its ruined rolling stock
to ride the rails another day,

the monument from which it plunged
unwary through the chasm of the gale:
those stubs of pillars strung across the Tay.

Julie Kennedy

BURKA

To hide
in a dark tent, not crawl
from under a hangover's stone
for a pint of milk, a loaf for toast.

That time
my brother died
I could have kept secret
the tides of my face.
I'd have taken a walking coffin.

I cannot get under its cloth.

I try a sheet at Halloween,
two holes cut out.
Play peek-a-boo with the cat
who knows me by my eyes.

Sunshine,
folk sipping latte
outside Costa Coffee:
'she must be roasting …'
'… looks dead sad … in the eyes.'

Flashing
the longest false lashes
they've ever seen,
she disappears to her part of the city.

Linda McCann

THE OLD MAN

For Philip Hobsbaum

A fresh flannel prairie buttoned on a bone-cage;
hand-me-downs from the man he used to be.
In a loosening drift of spent seasons he sits like a foxed
puppet being unfankled from above, blue stripes drawn
around him like brackets. Give you the Belsen horrors.

Curtain down, Queen saved, lights up. Quick.
Aground in the now, he pitches to his feet. She shoulders
him, calls him Dad, clutches a wishbone elbow and tillers
a twisted rhubarb arm where a fair lady smiles
and the muscles used to bulge like a neckful of spinach.

He toddles in a nappy to nowhere, up past his
die-by date; into extra time and no chance of winning.
He tells her: 'Christ, if I stood on a Hauf Croon
I could tell you whither it was heids or tails'.
An hourglass wrist ticks the dull pulse of a skindeep ocean
as the blue indelible boat sails into a bedsore sunset.

Marcas Mac an Tuairneir

ORANGE

Why the outcry,
Orangeman?
Why the hullabaloo
On Saturday afternoon,
When I'm eating my supper?

If you're so fond
Of the hue,
Would you plant a pip
In the earth and wait
For the blessing of life
To burst from the burial?

Would you write a sonnet
To the great circle of the sun,
Instead of your silk to put on,
Your shirt and fancy Sunday shoes?

You'd be happy then;
With a faceful of juice
And the fruit in your hand.

You'd not pay attention
To the wail-song of chanter.
You'd be too grateful,
To celebrate murder.

And thus, you'd be connoisseur
Of the vigorous roots of your tree
And you'd see the pasture
From which they grow, not verdant,
But enchanted and evergreen.

Marcas Mac an Tuairneir

ÒR-UBHAL

Carson do chaismeachd,
Fhir bhuidhe?
Carson do chlambraid
Air feasgar Disathairne
Agus mise ag ithe mo dhìnneir?

Ma tha thu cho dèidheil
Air an dath,
Nach cuir thu sìol san ùir
Is nach fuirich thu
Ri beannachd beatha
Bòrcadh bhon uaigh?

Nach dèan thu dàn
Do chearcall mòr na grèine,
An àite sròl a chur ort 's do leine
'S do bhrògan spaideil Sàbaid?

Bhiodh tu sona, an uair sin;
Le beul loma-làn sùgha
Is a' chnuasach nad làimh.

Cha toireadh tu an aire
Do ghlaodh is ceòl pìoba.
Bhiodh tu ro shòlasach son
Comharrachadh an aoig.

Is mar sin, bhiodh tu eòlach
Air freumhan treun do chraoibhe
Is chitheadh tu nach eil am feur
Bhom fàs iad gorm,
Ach seunta agus sìor-uaine.

WIRELESS

Morning.
My father,
With razor,
In the bathroom
And steam from the shower
Stifles the murmur
Of the wireless.

At night.
Bent over a board
In the dining-room,
Fine brush
Between fingers.

Listening
To *The Archers*.
Adding tint and moustache
To tin soldiers.

Fiddle music;
'Barwick Green'
And the fishy whiff
Of the rickety lamp.

Saturday afternoon.
On the way back
From drama class.
Deciding
Desert Island Discs.
Da-da-dah
  Da-da-dah
    Da-da-da-da-di-dah.

CAGAR-ADHAIR

Madainn.
M' athair,
Le ràsair,
Anns an t-seòmar-amair
Agus smùid bhon fhras
A' bàthadh mànran
A' chagair-adhair.

Air an oidhche.
Crom, aig bòrd
An t-seòmair-bhìdh,
Le bruis mheirbh
Eadar meuran.

Ag èisteachd
Ris na h-*Archers*.
A' cur datha is staise
Air saighdearan staoine.

Ceòl na fìdhle;
'Barwick Green'
Is fàileadh iasgail
An lampa aosmhoir.

Feasgar Disathairne.
A' faighinn air falbh
Bho chlasaichean dràma.
A' beachdachadh
Air Clàran an Fhàsaich.
Da-da-dà
    Da-da-dà
        Da-da-da-da-di-dà.

Christopher Whyte

AT A GRAVE THAT ISNA THARE

Már egy hete csak a mamára
gondolok mindig, meg-megállva.
—ATTILA JÓZSEF

Gin you haed a grave, I wad gang thare,
but efter the praise, the fyke, the lowe,
whan thay brocht whit wis left – naething but
a puir haundfu o stour – up til the hoose,
my faither didna hae onie idea

whit ti dae wi it, an in the end,
athoot sayin a word ti oniebodie,
he sent it back til the black trader's
an naebody spak aboot it again.
Syne, I canna gang an fin you thare

at your grave, thare's nae gairden, nae muir,
nae polisht heid-stane, nae slab, nae place
whaur I can lay this wechty burden doun,
this trauchle o words an thochts, e'en feelins,
sae that it cuid bless a wee bit grun,

consecrate it an, syne, mak it guid,
as you ligg aneath it. I ken thir
isna the words you'd expect ti hear
whan a son – e'en the yingest o the three
she cairriet in her wame an gied birth til –

spaeks ti his mither. But sin you'r deid
my tongue ocht ti hae its lowsin-time
an thare shuid be nae tether haudin back
its eloquence nou: a chield that speirs
the deid maun tell the truith, an I am feart.

Crìsdean MacIlleBhàin

AIG UAIGH NACH EIL ANN

Már egy hete csak a mamára
gondolok mindig, meg-megállva .
—ATTILA JÓZSEF

Nam bitheadh uaigh agad, rachainn fhìn thuic'.
Ach na dh'fhàgadh dhìot an dèidh nan òraid,
an dèidh na h-anshocair gu lèir 's an teine,
nuair a thug iad gus an taigh e, dòrlach
truagh a dhuslach, cha robh fhios aig m' athair

dè bu choir dha dhèanamh leis, 's mu dheireadh
thall, gun dad a ràdh ri neach sam bith,
thug e air ais don fhear-adhlacaidh e,
is cha do bhruidhneadh tuilleadh air a' chùis.
Mar sin, chan urrainn dhòmhsa dol a thadhal

air t' uaigh-sa, chan eil gàrradh ann no sliabh,
chan eil clach shnasaicht' ann, no leac, no àite
far am b' urrainnear a leagail sìos,
an t-eallach seo a dh'fhaclan, smuainteannan,
a dh'fhaireachdainnean cuideachd, 's dòch', gu bhith

'na mhathachadh do phìos beag talaimh, 's tu
nad laighe fodha. Tha iad eadar-dhealaicht',
na briathran a bhiodh dùil aig neach a chluinntinn
an uair a bhruidhneas mac, ge b' e am fear
a b' òige dhen an triùir a rugadh leatha,

ri mhàthair fhèin. A-nis, is tusa marbh,
cha bu chòir gu robh cuibhreach sam bith
a' bacadh fileantachd mo theanga, oir
feumaidh neach a bhruidhneas ris na mairbh
an fhìrinn uile inns'. Tha eagal orm.

The saicret that the twa o us shared,
alang wi my faither, cuid ne'er be
pit inti words – I haed an keepit it
in the wey that bairns daes athoot e'en
kennin it wis thare. It wis the cunyie,

the stane that haudit ilka constellation
in aa the braid heivins in its place.
Binna it wis thare the elements
wad hae been fechtin thegither ay,
till the lest day an thare'd be nae wey

thay cuid be reconciled ti ane anither
or pit back til thair ordinar wark.
That saicret wis the essence o the warld
– an it wis evil. A bairn canna
imagine onie warld ither nor

the ane whaur he wis born. Syne you cuid say
that evil wis the first lesson I lairnt
frae you, my mither, or frae youse baith.
An it wis wretchit. Evil isna glorious,
it isna great nor stately. Whan it kythes

guisin in that claiddin it appears
aa mixt up wi ither elements,
cause that is juist whit evil desires
mair nor onie virtue it cuid hae,
ti byde athoot a name, unrecognised.

An rùn-dìomhair a bh' againn, aig an dithis
dhinn agus aig m' athair, cha do ghabh e
dealbhachadh am faclan, bha e agam
air an dòigh a bhitheas aig na pàistean,
gun fhios agam gu robh e ann. Bha e

'na bhonn-stèidh aig an t-saoghal, no 'na cholbh
a chumas farsaingeachd na h-iarmailt làin
'na h-àite fhèin. Mura robh esan ann,
bhitheadh na h-eileamaidean uil' a' strì
ri chèile fad na sìorraidheachd, cha bhiodh

dòigh ann air an rèiteachadh, no 'n cur
a-rithist gus an obair ghnàthaichte.
Is e bun-bhrìgh na firinneachd a bh' anns
an rùn, is bha e olc. Cha smaoinich pàiste
air saoghal a tha eadar-dhealaichte

bhon t-saoghal anns an d' rugadh e. Mar sin,
faodar a ràdh gur e an t-olc an ciad
leasan a dh'ionnsaich mise bhuat, no bhuaibh.
Is bha e dìblidh. Chan eil an t-olc glòrmhor,
mòralach no stàiteil. Nuair a nochdas

e sa chòmhdach ud, is ann a thèid
a choimeasgadh le eileamaidean eile,
oir 's e na tha an t-olc ag iarraidh, thar
gach feairt a dh'fhaodadh a bhith aige, fantainn
neo-ainmichte, nach dèan neach aithneachadh.

Gin you speir at me aboot the face
o evil, I winna say the ane
a leader haes, a dictator wi
an airmie in his thrall, onie weel-kent face,
e'en a murderer's, ane that you see

in the newspapers an naebodie
can dout the wickitness o its wark,
but ane ilka-day an ordinar,
the face o the man that sells the papers,
or spaeks ti a neibor aa aboot

the wey the weather chynges as thay wait
on the bus thegither in the queue.
Or mibbie your ain face. My mither's face.
Gin you war gied anither chance ti spaek
efter the final dumbness that ay comes

you cuidna cry me fause nor say a word
agin whit I maun say ti you theday
cause evil is a kin o unnerstaunin,
a kennin that canna juist be pit by
the wey a bodie can pit by his claes.

It clings ilka bit as closely til
the fowk that is evil's sacrifice,
that kennin, as it daes til the anes
that became the instruments o evil.
Wha wad think unlairnin an forgettin

Ma dh'iarrar orm gu dè a' ghnùis bhios aig
an olc, cha fhreagrainn gur h-i 'ghnùis aig ceannaird
stàit, air neo ceann-feadhn' àraidh is arm
fo smachd, no gnùis sam bith tha ainmeil,
eadhon an tè aig murtair nochdas anns

na pàipearan-naidheachd, is nach fhaod teagamh
a bhith aig duin' air aingidheachd a ghnìomh',
ach gnùis tha dìreach coitcheann, cumanta,
gnùis an fhir a bhios a' reic nam pàipear,
mar eisimpleir, no chanas ri a nàbaidh

mar a tha an t-sìde caochlaideach,
is iad a' feitheamh air a' bhus sa chiudha.
No do ghnùis fhèin, is dòcha. Gnùis mo mhàthar.
Nam faigheadh tu a-rithist cothrom cainnt
às dèidh na balbhachd do-sheachaint' a thàinig,

cha b' urrainn dhut mo bhreugnachadh, no dad
a ràdh an aghaidh na thuirt mi a-nis,
bhon a tha an t-olc 'na sheòrsa tuigsinn,
eòlas nach urrainnear a chur air falbh
gu sìmplidh mar gum b' e pìos aodaich bh' ann.

Bidh e teannachadh dìreach cho rag
ris a' chuid a tha 'nan ìobairt dha,
an t-eòlas sin, 's a theannaicheas e ris
na bha 'nan ionnsramaidean aig an olc.
Cò chreideadh idir gur dòigh air fàs slàn

coud e'er be a wey o growin hail?
Shuid I, syne, forget aboot you nou?
The daily ritual o evil wis
pairt o the baun atween you an me,
that strang baun atween ilka mither

an her son. Gin it was like a gairment,
that normality, thae ordinar weys,
it's a gairment that you chuise for me,
an I got wrapt aroond me as a wean,
aamaist as close as my ain fragrant skin.

Wha buir the greatest blame? Wis it the man
that neglectit you an abuised me?
You cuid say thare wis nae link at aa
atween us, cause he wis unreachable
aa throu my bairnhuid, wi pyntit words,

wi cauld, crabbit weys an wi the scunner
that bydit wi him, like the myndin
that the bairns haes whan the pantomime
is feinisht, o the hingie's black claes,
or his cruikit face (tho whit happent

atween us wisna a play at aa).
Somewhaur richt in the hert o that knot,
in the intricacy, whaur the threids
comes thegither an is interwoven,
love haed been taigelt tae. Cause a bairn

a th' anns an do-ionnsachadh 's an dìochuimhn'?
Am bu chòir dhomh, air shàillibh sin, do chur
fo dhìochuimhne? Bha gnàthachas an uilc
'na phàirt dhen bhann a bh' eadar mis is tus',
am bann cho làidir th' ann eadar gach tè

's a mac. Nan robh e coltach ri pìos aodaich,
an àbhaisteachd, an cleachdadh gnàthaicht' ud,
b' e aodach e a roghnaich thu, 's a fhuair mi
air a phasgadh umam, 's mi 'nam leanabh,
ach beag cho dlùth rim chraiceann cùbhraidh fhìn.

Cò aig a bha am prìomh-chiont? Aig an fhear
bha ga do dhearmad, is a rinn mo mhàbadh?
Dh'fhaodte a ràdh nach robh ceangal sam bith
eadarainn, on a bha e cho do-ruighinn
air fad mo leanabais, le fhaclan sgeigeil,

le mhodhan fuara 's leis an sgreamhalachd,
an t-uabhas a lean dlùth ris, mar a' chuimhne
bhios aig na pàistean, is an pantomaim
air crìochnachadh, air aodach dubh a' chrochair'
no air a ghnùis fhiar (ged nach b' e dealbh-chluich

idir na thachair eadar esan 's mise).
An àiteigin an cridhe an t-snaidhm sin,
anns an ioma-lùbachd, measg nan snàthainn
a' coinneachadh le chèil' 's gan eadar-fhighe,
chaidh an gaol cuideachd a ribeadh. Oir

canna leuk upon the warld he sees
aroond him athoot feelin love for it.
Love is the mortar that bynds the bricks
o the hoose he uises thaim ti bigg,
the biggin o reality, whate'er

material the bricks thairsels is made frae.
Gin I haedna loved youse baith, my parents,
naething wad hae happent as it did.
The peitie I felt for you, my mither,
wis as braid as onie continent,

but ilka time I got a keek at you
your ship wis in the herbor, you on deck
aboot ti laeve – I cuid reach you nane.
The bairn isna ti blame for the abuiss
that he tholes, nor for the love he feels

for the abuisers that ruined an fyled him.
Gin I was staunin at that bairn's grave
insteid o at a grave that isna thare
an will ne'er be, the grave o a wumman
that dee'd sax year syne, I dinna ken

for shuir whit words wad rise ti my lips.
But that bairn is still alive theday
that you cuidna dowse aa thegither,
ay bydin in a corner o my bodie,
an that love is still alive an aa

chan urrainn do phàiste a bhith sealltainn
air an t-saoghal 's gaol a dhìth air. Tha
an gaol 'na aol-tàthaidh chumas ri chèile
breigean an taigh a thèid a thogail leis,
taigh na fìrinneachd, ge b' e an stuth

às am bi na breigean air an dèanamh.
Mura robh gaol agam oirbhse, air
mo phàrantan, bhiodh gach rud eadar-dhealaicht'.
Bha e cho farsaing ri mòr-roinn, na bha
mi faireachdainn de thruacantas mud dheidhinn,

ach gach uair a fhuaras plathadh dhìot,
bha thu anns an acarsaid, air bòrd
luinge, deiseil gu falbh, is tu do-ruighinn.
Chan e am pàiste 's coireach ris a' mhàbadh
a dh'fhuiling e, no ris a' ghaol a bh' aige

air an fheadhainn a thruaill is a mheall e.
Nan robh mi 'na mo sheasamh ri taobh uaigh
a' phàist', an àite uaighe nach eil ann,
's nach bi ann chaoidh, aig boireannach a chaochail
sia bliadhn' air ais, chan eil mi cinnteach dè

na faclan bhiodh ag èirigh gu mo bhilean.
Ach tha e fhathast beò, am pàiste ud
a dh'fhairtlich oirbh e fhèin a mhùchadh buileach,
a' còmhnaidh ann an ceàrn dhem bhodhaig fhìn,
is tha e beò cuideachd, an gaol a bh' aige

that he haed for his parents, that wis
decreitit til him as he wis til thaim,
bi the juidgement wi nae trace o care
for the speirin that ay oppresses us.
Gin you haed your ain ditch than mibbie

I cuid throwe ilka black jasp intil it,
the worry, the sel-hate an the guilt,
aa the heirship that you left ti us
sae you cuid tak thaim wi you on your journey.
But, sin I canna gang til your grave.

sin I hinna the strenth or the hate
I'd need ti forget you aa thegither,
I wish wi aa the pouer that I hae:
gin no my thanks, than my lest blessin
micht reach you in a place whaur you ar no.

For a week nou, aa I can think aboot
is my mither, it gars me stert.
—ATTILA JÓZSEF

Owerset bi Niall O'Gallagher

air a phàrantan, an dithis thug
binn àraidh dha, mar a thug is' e dhaibh,
a' bhinn nach eil lorg air cùram aice
thaobh nan ceist a bhios gar claoidheadh daonnan.
Nan robh clais shònraicht' agad, dh'fhaodainn, 's dòcha,

na leugan dubha ud a chàradh innt',
an t-iomagain, a' ghràin ort fhèin, an ciont,
an oighreachd uil' a dh'fhàg thu dhuinn, air dòigh
's gun rachadh iad air t' astar 'na do chuideachd.
A chionn 's nach fhaod mi dhol gu t' uaigh, a chionn 's

nach eil gu leòr a neart agam, no fuath,
's gun dèan mi do dhìochuimhneachadh gu tur,
's e dùraigeadh a h-uile chomas th' agam
gum faod mo bheannachd, mura b' e mo thapachd,
do ruighinn ann an àite far nach eil thu.

O chionn seachdain chan urrainn dhomh smaointinn
ach air mo mhàthair, bacaidh siud mo cheum.
—ATTILA JÓZSEF

Ian McDonough

SKY ABOVE TRAVELODGE, DUMFRIES

Smudged moon, smudged
stars. Smudgy clouds
passing over smudged
moon and stars.

The receptionist's thoughts
are smudgy too.
What's the name of yon soup
you make from beetroot?

And who was that fellow
Janice was devouring
last night?

On the smudged moon
an abandoned
space landing vehicle
blinks on through the darkness,
saying and thinking nothing,
relaying clean numbers
to a deaf and dirty world.

James McGonigal

WASHING LINES

1.

Evening; and sunset spills
its cup of juices
down the sky's blue chin.
I take the washing in,
unpegging scents of air and grain
in blouses, shorts, folded away
to breathe on children's skins: familiar
effort, intimate and everyday.

Long days to bleach our pillows clean
of sweat-stains and tears.
August bakes damp feathers dry –
still they won't fly.
Take them in too. It's time to fall
asleep at last.
Moth wings round a cooling lamp
beat for their vanished past.

2.

Ms Mona Lisa with her head thrown back –
new upstairs neighbour with a laugh so fierce
it cracks her floorboards and my cornices.

She loves entertaining friends.
She can cook up a storm.
Tonight it's Guffaw Flambé with crudités
serving 8 till late
from the genial dish of her face.

At weekends it's hung-over hellos
on the communal drying green.
We peg out pyjamas on separate lines
and leave them doubled over there

tears of laughter helplessly
dripping from each sleeve.

3.

Wet garments – the weight in them.
She carries her basket out into
midsummer – grandchildren's clothes.

Did you see the sun
hanging above the Campsie Fells
an hour before midnight?

Holiday shirts and jerseys shaken into light.
It's best to persevere but oh, with bent shoulders
and hands that dip and rise

to a breeze that lets everything go.

David Shaw Mackenzie

WHO BETTER?

'Who better to be you than you?' Kinnoul said to Telman. He was asking Telman to play himself in a film about his own life. 'Depends which me you want,' Telman said and they all laughed.

Telman was fifty-four then and had been out of office for two years following heavy defeat in 2031 in the elections prompted by the McLintock affair. They said his age was no problem; they could make him up to look like the man he'd been at thirty-nine when he'd got the top job. First, they'd teach him how to act.

It amused him to think he was learning to be himself. They taught him how to walk, how to stand, how to speak, how to hold a silence and he said, 'But that's not how I did it when I was there.' His amusement edged towards concern.

They didn't understand what he was worried about. It was Kinnoul who spoke to him. 'You asked us a question once,' he said. 'Right at the beginning. Do you remember?'

'What question was that?'

'"Which me do you want?"' Kinnoul said and he smiled. 'Remember?'

'Not really, no.'

'Well, it was a good question,' Kinnoul went on, 'and the answer is that we want you to be the you you would have been if you'd known then the things we're teaching you now.' And he left Telman to think about that.

Which he did. He went home and thought again about who he was, who he'd been, who he might yet be, who or what he wanted to be. And none of this was new. These were things he'd thought about for as long as he could remember thinking about anything. As usual, the problem lay in reaching a single conclusion. As before there were twenty-five or twenty-six of them.

*

He got a surprise when he read the script for the first time. He didn't recognise himself. There was the name – Sacheveral Telman (and spelt correctly, too) – but that was the only thing about this character that was true. And most of the others – members of his cabinet, family friends, other political figures – the names were all there but the people themselves were barely recognisable. There were changes, too, to the actual events.

'I never went to Ethiopia in 2027,' he said to Kinnoul.

'Didn't you?'

'No. I've never been to Ethiopia.'

'You would have gone, though, wouldn't you?' Kinnoul said. 'If you'd had the chance?'

'That's just it. I didn't have time. I was waist deep in domestic issues. There was the Progress Tax, for example, which … which you don't seem to mention at all.'

'Not very cinematic. In fact, very dull indeed. Now Ethiopia was different. People loved it because it was interesting. Starving kids, lots of deaths. You know, very cinematic.'

'But I never went there.'

'But you would have, if all that Progress Tax stuff hadn't messed it up,' Kinnoul insisted. 'You would've gone, wouldn't you?'

'Possibly.'

'Possibly?'

'All right, probably. Yes, I wanted to go and I probably would have gone.'

'You see,' Kinnoul said, 'we just take out the bits about the Progress Tax and allow you to do what you would have done anyway.'

He let it pass. He still had a problem with it but later he was to view it as a small problem, smaller anyway than the big problem he faced when they introduced him to the rest of the cast.

He asked to see Kinnoul privately.

'You've got to be kidding,' Telman said.

'Kidding? About what?'

'The Foreign Secretary, Millner.'

'Millner, yes. What about him?'

'He's black.'

'That's right. Lucas Fangle.'

'But you can't do this.'

'He's an excellent actor,' Kinnoul pointed out.

'He's black,' Telman repeated.

'I know he is. You're not prejudiced, are you?'

'No, I damn well am not. And you know I'm not. But Lucas … Lucas Tangle …'

'Fangle.'

'Fangle. Yes, he's black and my Foreign Secretary, Jack Millner, wasn't black, he was white. You can't go changing the colour of people's skin.'

Kinnoul shook his head. 'Well, it's all about quotas.'

'Quotas?'

'Yes. At least twenty-five percent of the actors have got to be of ethnic minority origin.'

'Even in a biopic when nearly all the actual people were white?'

'Exceptions aren't allowed.'

Telman laughed. 'Well, I don't believe it,' he said. 'Who the hell dreamt up that stupid law?'

'You did.'

'Me?'

'Don't you remember? The Labour Levelling Law of 2028.'

'Christ, it was never meant to be anything like this.'

'Well, it is like this. We've got quotas now and we stick to them. Otherwise we'd be breaking the law. Your law.'

Telman said nothing for a few seconds. Then he stood up. 'This is ridiculous,' he said at last. 'And I quit.' He left the room.

*

But soon he was back. Kinnoul needed to explain a few things to him.

'First, we're already quite a way into production and it's too late for you to quit. Then there's the question of your contract.'

Telman said, 'I've signed nothing so far.'

'Well, you may believe that you've signed nothing but the nothing you've signed is a contract with me.'

'I've never seen a contract,' Telman said.

'So, you had your eyes shut when you signed it. I can assure you that I've got a copy, my lawyer's got a copy and if you walk out now I'll sue you for all the money you've got and a whole lot more besides.'

'Now just a—'

'Shut up!' Kinnoul shouted and Telman was shocked. When was the last time someone had told him to shut up? Kinnoul paused, then continued, quietly, 'Let me tell you why you really want to make this movie, why you really, really, really want to make this movie.'

'Oh yeah? And why's that?'

Kinnoul smiled and then said just one word: 'McLintock.'

Telman leaned back in his chair and folded his arms.

Kinnoul went on, 'As far as the McLintock business is concerned, let me tell you what really happened.'

'You mean, in the film,' Telman said.

'Yes. What really happened.'

And Kinnoul told him the story, from beginning to end, in great detail, and Telman was amazed because he hadn't realised what had really happened. McLintock, after all, was not a man who had exposed a level of bribery and corruption in Telman's government the like of which had never been seen in British politics before. Quite the reverse, McLintock was a self-aggrandising, scheming, manipulating, cheating bastard, the very lowest of the low, whose lies and deception had brought down the best government Britain had ever had.

*

The film was made, with Telman's full participation. It made a lot of money but the critics didn't like it much. One remarked that although the film was historically accurate, Telman was no good at being himself. Someone else, with more acting talent, would have done a better job – someone like Lucas Fangle, for example, who was first rate as Foreign Secretary Jack Millner.

Nevertheless, Telman was nominated for an Oscar. He didn't win.

Kirsten MacQuarrie

PENTIMENTI

At 8:14 she begins to type. Her job is straightforward. The university archive is underground, hidden in the shadows beneath shining under-grad prospects and strip-lit, tenured ambition. Every day she passes the rucksacks and briefcases of street level and burrows down into this secure, rhythmic world; secluded by oak panels and lamplight, she can concentrate. Though her world lacks colour for it, after once being cowed by the darkness of fear it is in certainty that she finds refuge. Sepia for survival: a bargain made ten years ago.

She records other people's words about other people's pictures. *Softly modelled, Ramsay's exquisite portrait exudes a sympathetic grasp of character* ... states one exhibition catalogue, a glossy folder wrapped in duck-egg blue. *Softly modelled, Ramsay's exquisite portrait exudes a sympathetic grasp of character* ... she types. *A little-known and intensely individual painter, Pringle captures a luminous effect* ... reads another: this one smaller, cubic and awkward. *A little-known and intensely individual painter, Pringle captures a luminous effect* ... she types. It did not take her long to understand the job. Didn't take any of them long. Except, perhaps, Sandra. 'No one hears from her these days since she moved back in with her mother' Sandra. *'Hark the Herald Angels Sin'* Sandra. Except perhaps Sandra.

The computer cursor flickers. Her keyboard clicks. Time passes and she starts to feel safe. Then the phone rings.

'Where are you?' His voice is metallic (the subterranean reception is poor, which she enjoys) with a slight, static delay.

'Hello, Adam. I'm at work.' *Where you knew I would be*, she thinks but does not say. He sounds distant; echoes shroud the line with grey impersonality and there is another noise too: the soft crackling of raindrops. She imagines (the archive has only one window, above her head: during lunch she watches people's feet) clouds on the horizon, shading the landscape with a thin veil of charcoal.

'What are you doing?' She looks at the photograph before her. The painting – another Pringle – shimmers on the page, the ethereal medley of dots whispering its possession of a single moment in time. She will keep it to herself.

'Abstract Expressionism,' she lies. Adam sneers. He hates abstraction. *I could have done that*, he always says. *But you didn't*, she never says.

'I've just been to the church,' he tells her. Down the tunnel of the phone line she hears his feet crunching on gravel. Quick. Tinny. Irritated. And the other sound: the sound of the rain. She imagines the chill in the air, the silvery knowing glint of a storm about to break.

'Is it still raining?' she asks.

'What?'

'Is it still raining?'

'Well, yes, now that you mention it.' She can hear him looking around. He is often surprised that elements outwith himself can change.

'I don't mind the rain. I think ...'

'Shut up, Frances.' The strike came through tone, not volume, but still it resonates. The space fills with the sound; his voice clings to the walls, creeping upwards until the whole room is smothered. In the moments that pass a few tendrils remain: they reach out for her, jealous and cloying. It is strange to hear her name in that way. She looked it up once. *Frances, meaning freedom*. In the archive window the feet and paws of a dog and its walker are briefly visible: both waterlogged, both melancholy.

Clip. Frances starts. Clip. Clip. Clip. A colleague (the newest one, with the highest heels, who never arrives before 9:07) has walked up to the desk. The corner of her blouse hangs outside her waistband, a tiny origami fold propped defiantly against her hip. Her make-up is approximate; a smear of pink streaks merrily across her lips. And when she smiles she glows, in a way Frances recognises only from artwork. She is miming something. *When, finished, coffee, we, go?*

'Frances,' says Adam. Frances thinks of coffee shared: the warm enveloping smell of roast, the comforting hiss of steam. The talking about their lives.

'Frances,' says Adam. Frances shakes her head. Her colleague's eyes cloud for a moment with something Frances cannot quite decipher. Then she nods, shrugs, and turns away.

'Did you hear me, Frances? I was at the church. They said the deposit hasn't been paid.' She looks down. The knuckles of her left hand, furled into a fist some seconds earlier, have paled. Her ring is cut sharply and even, uncompromisingly symmetrical, but the light is too low for the diamond to shine.

'I told you to book it.' She twists the ring around her finger, the stone turning away and coming to rest slightly askew. For all its beauty (and expense, she knows: she can feel the weight it brings to her hand) at this angle it looks ugly; the imposing regularity – so classically desirable when seen from a certain perspective – now leers at her, soulless and grotesque.

'I know. I'm sorry.' It needs resized, but she won't tell Adam. It would only upset him. 'I'm sorry.'

Adam sighs. The rain sounds heavier. 'I want this wedding to be perfect.'

She replaces the phone and turns to the next catalogue. Abstract Expressionism. She almost smiles, and starts to type. But as she stares at the picture – an inkblot, large, black on white – she sees beyond the brushstrokes. She sees a black door. A handsome black wooden door, solid and varnished until passers-by could see themselves in it, should they ever choose to look. And behind it she sees herself. A child, slim and ashen, limbs quivering with fear and with rage she fights to supress. She sees her father, tall and suited, a man to be trusted. She sees her mother, on the floor, and a red line mixed of tears and blood trickling down her cheek. She sees the night ten years ago when she knew – even after the sirens, even after the strangers, even after being wrapped in a blanket that smelled of other children and being told that she was safe – life had changed. She sees the day the world turned black and white.

*

'*Edgar Degas,* The Rehearsal, *1873–4.*'

The visit was unplanned.

'*Executed in rapid strokes of pastel, this glimpse into a ballet studio articulates Degas' aim to "capture movement in its exact truth".*'

Her train broke down. Panic threatened to descend. So she walked, steps clipped and timed to her breathing (*One. Two. One. Two. Not. Today*), until arriving by chance at the museum.

'*His work investigates not only dance but the nature of motion: symbolic perhaps of life itself and its constant potential for change. Indeed, viewers may observe several areas where preliminary sketching – exploratory, experimental and above all imperfect – remains visible.'*

Why does she stay? She never dances.

'Far from being hidden, these imperfections are embraced as part of the piece's impact, and in fact are integral to the "truth" of Degas' movement. We call this technique—'

One minute longer.

'—pentimenti.'

*

Returning home, the rain has stopped. She eats her evening meal. Eats a little extra. Then she takes out the paints. Dust has left a sheen; she blows gently and a haze of particles glitters before her eyes. The phone goes. She ignores it. She removes her ring, and begins. There are mistakes, many of them, but with trembling hands she continues, effort upon effort as evening becomes nightfall. The sunset moves from coral, to umber, to the pure beam of moonlight – and she is illuminated.

Ian Madden

HURRYING HANDBAGS TO KYLEAKIN

The Veich was the biggest liar on the Isle of Skye. This ancient crofter – our nearest neighbour – was so scandalous that my father would not mention him until my younger brother and I were abed. As a seven-year-old I heard about the doings of this snowy-whiskered rogue only when sitting out of sight at the top of the stairs. My mother would be mending socks by the fire. Opposite her my father gouged and scraped at the bowl of his pipe.

'Do you know what that scoundrel did today, Mary?'

It wasn't just the Veich. The whole family was at it – his daughter and his grandson. Whatever you had, they had one better. Whatever you might have done, they'd done it ages ago. That time a plane flew low over the village and everyone talked about it for weeks, only one man was favoured by a smile and a wave from the pilot.

In March 1951 my father was laid up with a fever so I had to take on the running of the croft. I was nearly sixteen. My grandfather was on hand to pass comment. Thankfully he didn't live with us but that didn't stop him from turning up every day. We spoke Gaelic at home, my grandfather making it sound less like a language than one long adverse judgement: 'That boy is the most cack-handed creature I have ever seen. The clumsiest in living memory ...' No good at digging, uneasy with the beasts; what was to be done with me? To add insult to injury, I'd been named for my mother's father. Fearsome as he was, this stung him. He made it his business to see about having my name swapped with my brother's. He'd even written to a government office in Edinburgh enquiring how to go about this.

With defects like mine, how would I earn a living? Even I didn't know the answer to that. If you went by the whitewashed stone pronouncements I was brought up among, clumsiness could have been something objected to in Leviticus. At that time and in that place any perceived fault had biblical roots and penalties: it could have led to eternal damnation. Most things did.

Luckily my father was back at work within the week and things returned to normal. However, one day – just before he got his strength back – stands out as the clearest, most decisive, least clumsy day of my life.

*

Flour on her arms, the Veich's daughter Kenna – herself well into her sixties – came into our kitchen early one morning calling out for my father. She was ashen. On hearing her, my mother appeared in the doorway. Later my mother said she half expected Kenna to claim that one of her family was in a worse state than my father; and to be cadging medicine. She said she had felt like cautioning the woman to tell the truth for once. Then Kenna spoke.

Not even she would lie about such a thing.

*

When I was sure my younger brother was asleep, I'd get out of bed and creep to the top of the stairs and hope to hear something interesting. There were no wireless sets in those days. Or rather, there *were* but we didn't have one. Anyway, these tales of the Veich's doings had everything the BBC would have provided: current affairs, education and public information. As well they had something not offered by the wireless: stories without a moral.

'He shouted to me this morning from behind the flock of sheep he was driving to the moorland.' Without seeing him, I knew my father was now putting pipe to mouth and clenching it between his teeth the better to impersonate the Veich, '"I see Hitler's no' been doin' badly …"' There was a pause. 'It's all the same to that man, Union Jack or Swastika. What difference does it make to him what flag's flying in London as long as he has sheep to sell to the butcher?'

You could almost hear my mother at her darning.

'He's amoral, Mary. Not immoral. Amoral.'

Unseen on the top stair, with your feet near freezing, there's no word quite as wonderful as one you don't know the meaning of – but can have a good guess at.

*

'Where's the "v"?' I asked my mother. I'd mastered the alphabet and was learning to spell.

'There's no "v" in Gaelic. Well, there's one in the dictionary but we don't use it. What's so important about "v"?'

I told her.

She sighed. 'It's "*bh*" you've been hearing.'

But it was too late. 'The Veich' he had always been. 'The Veich' he would remain. And why shouldn't such an accomplished borrower have a consonant filched (or on permanent loan) from a neighbouring language?

As a small child, it never occurred to me that the name by which he was known was not his real name. Everyone called his family the Veichs. I was almost school age when my father told me they had a surname as Scottish as ours. He explained that many years ago it was common for parents to give the same name to their children. That happened with our neighbour. His name was Murdo. His older brother's name was Murdo, too. Their father nicknamed one boy Murdo *mór* – big Murdo; and the other Murdo *bheig* – little Murdo. Even after the eldest child died aged ten their father continued calling his younger son *bheig*.

His very jacket spoke of skulduggery. Even when empty the pockets looked as if they contained a jam jar each. The stories I'd overheard about him coupled with his unwillingness to speak to a mere boy made me think of the Veich as remote, a picture-book illustration come to life. Who needed tales of walking the plank and rum smuggling when down the hill lived an octogenarian who 'would leave nothing lying he could lift'?

*

Chin on my knees, fingers squeezing my toes, I heard creaks, lowered voices and mystifying words – words I strained to catch. None were stranger than those my mother uttered when recounting what had caused her father never to speak of or to the Veich for the past twenty years: '*A cagnadh air a chas mhaide.*'

There was a knock. My guilty backside sprang off the top stair. Just as I was ready to scamper back to bed there was a series of rapid, sharper knocks. My panic ebbed. I sat down again. It was only my father rapping his pipe on the inside wall of the fireplace. I didn't have to be in the room to see it: how close his hand got to the flames, dried grey-white ash dropping from the upturned bowl and a ripped-looking film of soot fluttering against bare, almost clean, brick.

*

The only person for miles who had a telephone was Dr MacLeod. I was sent there to ring Mitchison the undertaker.

'Are you immediate family?' the voice demanded.

'No. The family came to see my father.'

'Why isn't he calling me?'

'He's ill.'

'Who's paying?'

'They are,' I guessed.

'How?' He left no time for another guess. 'Is there a policy?'

'I'm not sure.'

'Well find out. Why can't they speak to me themselves?'

'They're too upset.'

'Look. I'm away to the mainland later today. If they want a coffin this is what you do …' He mentioned the time of the ferry he was catching and said he'd be waiting in the lounge bar of the Marine Hotel at Kyleakin for half an hour or so before that. 'Bring a policy or the money to me there.'

*

When I got back from the doctor's, Kenna asked me to accompany her home. We didn't speak while we walked. I wanted to say something but couldn't think of anything. Kenna had her thoughts. I had mine. With my father sick and me doing the work, my mind had been dwelling for days on a single thought: not wanting to spend my life as a crofter. More, I wanted to leave Skye but didn't know how to tell my parents. On top of this, I wasn't sure what I *did* want to do.

Up past the sloping byres – which housed the beasts the Veich had been about to feed when it happened – a sheep veered from us and jolted at another with its shoulder. Both trotted away, incurious. As I strode towards it, I realised I'd never been inside their croft. I'd only ever been as far as the back door. Looming in the doorway was Willie, Kenna's son, the only button of his baggy jacket fastened in the wrong buttonhole.

'Is there a policy?' I asked.

The two of them looked at each other. And shook their heads.

'Mitchison says he'll need one or some money before he can make the arrangements.'

'He put something by whenever he could ...'

I didn't know whether to believe her.

In the middle of the floury table was a hulk of dough bearing the imprints of Kenna's knuckles. On the only chair in the kitchen a death certificate had been left. It was kept in place by a tin of potted meat. Dr MacLeod must have been and gone.

Kenna heaved her way into the room where her father's body lay; soft-whiskered, toothless, serene – all mischief gone. I pulled the eiderdown up over his face. After producing the biggest pair of scissors I'd ever seen, Kenna knelt down and began cutting open a stitched-up scar in the side of the mattress.

On the other side of the bed, her son set about doing the same. Willie watched what he was doing. His mother, though, kept her eyes on me. She pulled at the wool stitching. Then she stuck her arm inside the mattress, eventually coaxing from it something which looked like a partially defeathered cock pheasant. But it had handles. Whatever it was, Kenna dropped it on the bed. Willie hauled out something saggy, black and beaded and dropped it next to the other object.

Kenna slit a line of stitching for me. Wordlessly, I set about helping. Each of us groped – an elbow or sometimes even a shoulder disappearing as we did so – in the mattress until it was empty. When we finished there were more than a dozen handbags, no two the same, on the bedspread.

Willie picked up a scuffed bag of morocco leather and tipped out its contents by his grandfather's feet. Coinage of all descriptions cascaded on to the mantle: pennies, farthings, halfpennies, threepenny bits, sixpences and the occasional shilling.

'You think this'll be enough?'

I had no idea how much Mitchison would charge but not more than the combined contents of the bags, surely.

'I think so, Willie.'

'Will you pay the man?'

'How will I get to him before he leaves?'

'Your father's got a car.'

'He's in bed. He's too ill to drive.'

'Not him,' said Willie. 'You.'

*

Knolls of desolate rock sped by. Who was this man I was hurtling through the landscape to pay? I'd never set eyes on him. But I knew of him. It was said that soon after he took over from his father thirty-odd years ago, Mitchison had got into an argument outside a pub at closing time. The brawl became notorious for the reproach levelled by the then young undertaker in between swings at his foe, 'Your mother never paid for your father's coffin.'

Passing the dip in the road where years earlier I'd come across our old neighbour inspecting a drystone wall, I slowed down. He'd looked round at me then turned back to the wall and – without interrupting his perusal of the stones – ventured, 'There were some Americans here an hour or two ago.'

'Americans?'

'Aye. And they did no more than ask me whether this was the place where Bonnie Prince Charlie first set foot on Skye.'

'What did you say?'

'I said, "Not this exact spot." I pointed to that rock over yonder and told them, "There. That's where he stepped off the boat." They took photographs of it.'

'The very rock? I never knew that ...'

The old man had looked as if he shared my grandfather's opinion of me.

'They went away content,' he'd declared.

A steady drive to Kyleakin would have taken about two hours. But the roads were mine. I put into practice every rule of driving I'd been taught – only quicker. The car displayed a deftness it had never been called upon to show before. I had it all worked out; the story I'd tell if I was stopped by the police. Envisioning the scene, a brief explanation was all it would take to make the officer let me continue on my way. My age and my speed would have been overlooked once the kindly constable had been told of the reason for my haste: payment to Mitchison so he would dispatch his son to fit the Veich with a coffin.

A wide bend in the road led down to a stone bridge. Not far from here was where my grandfather's brother had lived. Back came the awful words, words wrapped in creaks and night sounds as my mother recalled how, in the late 1920s, her uncle had gone to the mainland for work, laying railway track. There he ate a square meal, day after day, for the first time in years. He had been away for a couple of years when he was involved in a terrible accident. The full meals came to an end. The railway gave him a tiny allowance and an artificial limb. And he came home. Poverty in those days was so dire that some in the village envied my great-uncle's plight. It was around this time that my grandfather broke off relations with the Veich after hearing him say of our family, *'They're all up there gnawing on the wooden leg.'*

*

Triumphant at getting to the Marine Hotel in good time, I carried as many of the bags as I could into the lounge bar. Walking backwards through the door, I turned to see the undertaker pouring what looked like a glass thimbleful of colourless liquid into a pint of black liquid. He held the thimble over the pint, waiting for the last drop to detach itself. In this position he looked up and said, 'Good Lord, boy. What have you got there?'

I set the bags on the bench beside him and explained.

Mitchison had a habit of touching – not wiping, just touching – the side of his mouth with the knuckle of his index finger as if to remove a crumb. I remained standing while he counted.

When at last the undertaker had got the amount he wanted the table was covered with careful piles of coins. Some still-fat handbags were on the bench to his left; those to his right had the look of thoroughly gutted rabbits. He did not comment on the inconvenience of the method of payment but merely let a smirk settle on his cadaverous face. He took a sip of his mysteriously fortified Guinness then enunciated through thin, frothless lips, 'Always get the money while the eyes are still moist.'

*

I'd had my story ready but I didn't need it. I didn't see a policeman. I saw almost no one. Should I have driven without a licence – and driven at such speed? Was it really necessary? It seemed so at the time.

Kyleakin was the furthest south I'd ever been. It was the *furthest* I'd been. Up until then, I'd been on the verge of believing what my grandfather said of me. The drive from the village to the ferry had offered the first notion that he may have been wrong. On the lazy drive home, I felt full of possibility. There was something I was fit for.

*

All the men for miles around were in the room. All, that is, except my grandfather. Tea was drunk from white pint pots. So was coffee. There was a strong wind that night. The room was full of the smell of smoke blown back down a chimney. It was the first staying-up I'd attended. On these occasions the family of the deceased usually got some sleep while neighbours sat with the coffin. Kenna had gone to bed. Willie stayed up.

I tried not to remember what I'd been told of the origins of the custom: originally it was so that the menfolk could prevent vermin getting at the body. Standing beside the hearth, my father wondered how the undertaker had transported his takings. How did Mitchison manage with all that loose change? We never found out. The pleasure to be had from quiet conjecture was better than any answer.

In the midst of this I told my father the job I wanted to do. He didn't object. So I went one further. I said I'd like to make my living on the mainland.

'Any place in particular?'

'MacLennan's in Inverness.'

'The furniture store?'

'Yes. It needs van drivers.'

By the way my father took that next mouthful of tea I knew there would be no fuss.

The croft was stark, smoky. The shiny pine casket was the most ostentatious object in the room.

'How old was he?' I asked.

'A year or two older than my father would've been.'

'How old's that?'

'Let's see, now. My father'd have been …' He took a slurp of very strong tea. 'He'd have been ninety-four next month.'

No sooner had he said this than I spotted the plaque on the coffin lid.

'I think you made a mistake, Pa.'

My father had a look. There it was, inarguable, in brass: 1851–1951.

'Maybe I did.' He raised his pint pot towards the departed. 'Or maybe the auld Veich isn't going to let a little thing like death get in the way of a long-standing family tradition.'

Susan Mansfield

BEARING SOUTH

I want answers, but there are only the wild geese
Calling, high in the almost-dark, bearing south,
And me, stopped short, clutching a bag of groceries
On the doorstep of my not-quite home.
I feel the calm of their inner compass
And wonder if this is what we mean by certainty,
A deft arrowhead of wingbeats
In tune with the turning wind, the changing light,
A geography in their feathery breasts
Older than the names of continents.
A journey without thought of parting or arrival,
Only the press of forward motion,
The urgency and risk of it all,
A brief touch-down in stubble fields, then on,
The pulse of fellow flyers in the slipstream
And the clear voices calling in the dark:
I am here, I am alive,
I am here, I am alive.

Duncan Stewart Muir

NOTES FOR SURVIVING

Beware the Leorin cow who broke
the farmer's boy against the dyke

and now has a taste for cracking bones.
Do not anger your brother, who is gentle

with children, tender with animals, but keeps
a streak of red rage, clenched

between his fists for you. Do not
approach the wild ponies, the yellow

reach of their teeth, their unshod hooves.
Don't follow deer tracks

down the abandoned mine shafts
where the bones of lost creatures litter

the loose brown earth. And when you kill,
be clean, remember that you should not

enjoy it, and always scrub the blood
from beneath your nails before school.

Ingrid Murray

DREAM 1

With first line after Derek Mahon

I too want to be
the one: to vanish
when the bell rings,

to turn my back
on everyone even
if they come calling.

In my dream I'd live
in a little house
by fields in corn.

A beck would run.
I'd keep a dog,
a small one with wiry hair.

The sun would shine
on alternate days.
The wet days I'd stay in,

read Plato,
learn the violin, bake bread,
stay thin.

From the ancient heart
you'd call my name
and I would answer

with an owl's hoot
so you would know
not to come

by the Law Road
but to wait for me at the foxes' den
till evening.

Niall O'Gallagher

UBHAL

Can a-rithist e, a mhic,
   agus e do chiad fhacal,
cluinneam air do theanga e,
   ainm a' mheasa as blasta:

ubhal. A dhà lide chruinn
   nam foghair fhuinn nad bheul-sa,
abair aon uair eile e,
   mar gur e briathair seunta

a bh' ann: *ubhal*. Gabh blas dheth
   's tu cho measail air, cumadh
do ghruaidh ruaidh, agus a dhath
   uaine air neo dearg: *ubhal*.

Rach don chraoibh airson am fear
   as milse, seirbh' a thogail
sìos, gabh do leòr, cuibhreann math
   dheth agus tu gad bhogadh

ann am brìgh nam faclan, sùgh
   na cainnt, an sùgradh taitneach,
sultmhor: *ubhal*. Coma leat,
   na toir aire do nathair

ann, na abradh nach ann dhut
   a tha gach fear dhiubh, furain
bhriathran, mheasan, fhuaimean gràidh,
   aicill as àille: *ubhal!*

FALACH-FEAD

Là bha siud bha mi a' cluich
    le ball a-muigh air an t-sràid
leis na gillean eile nuair,
    gu h-obann, ghluais duine àrd

a-steach bho ionad às còir,
    le gunna mòr dubh na làimh
gus an gabhadh esan breab.
    Bha e a' streap suas don àit'

pheanas a ghabhail ach leig
    mo ghranaidh fead 's i gam ghairm
a-steach don taigh is air falbh
    anns a' bhad bho fhear an airm.

Dh'fhalaich mi mi fhìn air cùl
    an t-sòfa, mo shùilean glact'
air a' bhulaidh mhòr a thug
    oirnn uile ar gèam' a stad.

Cha robh fios agam gun robh
    fear tron ath-dhoras a' cur
a gheugan air – ach a chuims'
    b' ann nam dhruim dheigheadh a' bhuill';

chan fhaca mi ach fear mòr
    a thug ar cuid spòrs gu crìch,
chan fhaca an gille beag
    làn eagail, coltach rium fhìn.

Louise Peterkin

SISTER AGNIESZKA RUNS AWAY TO THE CIRCUS

Roll up! Big-top in view like a yummy mirage;
scalloped, candy-striped, as good as any church
in scale, in height for the swooping,
the twirling, the leaping and curving
for the love of God, the love
of the falling. The good folk here
fit you for your leotard.
Instructed all day in the fine arts: juggling,
knife-throwing, tight-rope walking.
You know now balance
is an act of sheer faith,
so spread those arms out in the style of the cross
on a frail bridge above, on the back of a horse.
After work, there is much to enjoy –
a consignment of massive animals,
the Ark-stink of dark and straw.
Lie with the strong-man, all night long
if you care to, savour the taste of his body,
his shiny skin, his Colonel Blimp face.
Or console the associates of the side-show
as they hover towards your implicit grace, soothe them,
let the conjoined twins envelop you like a moth.
Be fearless as you walk that line,
straight across, don't look up or down.
And don't succumb to your nightmare –
you know the one –
where the ground, the trailers,
the skin of the tent tremble,
and you run outside to see

a legion of nuns
come to collect you
come to take you home
lapping at the horizon like an army of penguins,
in their vengeance, Sister,
in their thousands.

Peikko Pitkänen

DESERT

Children cry inconsolably and cling to their mothers' skirts with dirty hands. Something is always lost and never being found: socks, wellies, mittens. Milk spills, snot runs, and tears. In the playground wind throws dust into the eyes of the women who write messages in the sand: *Life is a desert, love is an illusion. I wish to be a goddess with ten pairs of legs and hands. Household duties are never-ending, our days are as long as supermarket corridors.* They say to each other: after ten or fifteen years we will come to an oasis and rest in the shade of a palm tree; until then the soundtrack of our lives is the drone of a washing machine. We snap our fingers and shake our hips while clothes spin inside a drum and bras wrap themselves around long johns. On the swings the children rise above the ochre wasteland like kites. In their bright-coloured rain suits they reach out to the stars and planets and smudge rainbows in the sky with finger paints.

Alison Rae

THE CURRY MOUSE

Saturday nights, while we sleep,
he sets out from base camp:
up the down pipe,
through the Gorge of Jif,
past Domestos Cliffs and
up the north face of his Everest –
grey, slippery, treacherous.

Does he wield a tiny pickaxe, his claws
four tiny crampons on his paws?
Does he use his tail as rope?

A summit lid-blocked,
and no TNT to blast the impasse,
he carves a pass of his own: teeth gnaw
a route through – the first clue for us to find.

He does not stop
to take a snap or plant a flag,
but orders a table for one and feasts
his eyes:
dhansak, bhuna, biryani,
the murine mountaineer's prize.

Belly swollen as
Dad's the night of the samosa sweats,
he rests,
reposed against a popadom rock,
digesting the view.

The bloated maharaja exits the Bombay Palace,
leaves an incontinent trail
from the subcontinent (our second clue)

back to base camp,
where he will find
the Alka-Seltzer that dropped behind
in 1972.

In the morning, while he sleeps,
I creep down stairs
to stand, feet bare
on cold linoleum,
eating the spice of life
straight from the fridge as distant bells
chime others to prayer.

Cynthia Rogerson

THE BACHELOR

He heard her car coming up his track. His head pounded and so did his heart, a dual of bongos. Without thinking, he switched off the lights. Locked the door, pulled the curtains. Ha! That would stop her! There he stood, alone in the dark kitchen. Her car stopped but nobody got out. He began to feel triumphant, though over what, he'd be embarrassed to say out loud. She was a nice woman. A well-liked, friendly woman – and after all, he'd found her company pleasing for at least six months. She didn't, as far as he knew, frighten anyone else. Certainly no one considered her a bunny-boiler. Her chocolate roulade was famous at the village hall sales, and last year it had even become a raffle prize. He understood these honours were not given lightly.

*

A car door opened, footsteps crunched gravel, then his door handle rattled. Jesus, was she a thief, as well as an undiscouraged ex-girlfriend? This was, indeed, pretty scary. He stopped breathing till the footsteps crunched back to the car. He stood still as stone, his heart hammering in his ears. Then the car rumbled off down the track again. He began to breathe normally. Smiled foolishly. Already, his fear seemed silly. He was reaching for the light switch when he heard a ... was it a cough? He froze, hand midway to the switch. There it was again. Definitely a cough, then a nose being blown.

She was on his porch.

He crept to the kitchen door, peeked into the darkened hall through to the glass front door. Sure enough, clearly illuminated by the porch light, there she stood. She turned around and appeared to be scanning the horizon. For him? She hugged herself as if she was cold. There must have been someone else in the car. She must have said: *Take my car. I'll wait here, he won't be long.*

The presumption! But that was one of the disadvantages of being a homebody. Not that he never left the house – every Tuesday afternoon he trawled the aisles of Tesco, and every Friday he walked to the pub for a pie and several pints with Tod.

Oh, what did she want?

He had nothing to give her, he'd been very clear. But then he recalled the kiss. He must stop drinking. Drink had led to the kiss in the pub's back corridor last Friday. All night long, he'd been aware of her presence in the lounge bar with her friends, and he'd sat in the public bar ignoring her. He occasionally heard her intoxicated laughter over the jukebox – the two rooms shared the same bar and barmaid. If he raised himself up a bit, he could even see the top of her head. He sat with Tod, talking of not much, or nothing he could remember. In fact he could remember nothing at all but that kiss.

She'd been heading to the toilet the same time he was.

'You! I didn't know you were here!'

'How have you been?' Well, he had to be civil, didn't he?

'Oh, great. Brilliant, in fact.' Then her face had crumpled and somehow ended up in his chest. Next thing he knew, it was like letting himself drop into the loch on a hot day. That same letting go, that not-thinking. She'd tasted of cider and lipstick. Probably he'd promised to ring her, and now here she was, standing on his porch like she lived here and forgotten her door key.

Well!

He could imagine slipping back into their old ways, and was tempted – even knowing he'd have to break up with her all over again one day. He had no idea how other men negotiated relationships. Women seemed so helpless in the beginning, and he liked the way they didn't care about winning or being clever. It was charming the way they laughed at themselves. Rapport always seemed effortless. You could tell a woman anything at this early stage, and they'd think you were absolutely normal, and more – wonderful and sometimes even funny. God, wasn't it great, to make a woman laugh? Forget orgasms, making a woman laugh was better. Not that the naked-in-bed bit wasn't good. That was the bit that always made him forget everything else.

But sooner or later the relationship would tip over into something less open, less comprehensible, less fun. He would end up yawning a lot, and making excuses to open windows and go for solitary walks.

*

He sighed and took a step towards unlocking the door. He'd tell her he'd not been well, had gone to bed early and not heard her knocking. It seemed inevitable they'd end up in bed. Friday night's kiss would demand that payment. Then she coughed again, and this time coughed up phlegm and expertly spat over the porch railings.

He froze. Felt himself gag. He'd never seen her when she'd not felt watched by him.

There was something vulnerable about her unawareness, but also something deeply unattractive. She looked slack, vacant. The skin just under her chin was crumply in a loose old-lady way, and the lines radiating out from her eyes were deep and dark.

He'd forgotten how old she was.

Then he watched, horrified, as she scrabbled about on his porch, lifting pots and feeling along the door frame.

'Yes!' she said, and slid his spare key into the lock.

*

He quickly reversed to the kitchen on tiptoes. Opened a low window and slipped out. It was raining; he'd not noticed before. She was already making herself at home. Turning on lights, music. He could hear water rushing. She was filling the kettle, cheeky thing! He crouched under the window in his tee shirt and jeans, getting wetter. She slid the window shut, but he could still hear her singing along to the music. He dared a peek. She was towelling her hair with his favourite towel – washed, folded and put away this morning. Her shoes had been kicked off in the middle of the floor and she was doing a little dance. He fancied it was a victory dance. Then she went to the other window looking out on to the track, and just stood there, as if looking for him could summon him. This moved him because she reminded him of a dog he had when he was a boy. That same intense patience and optimism.

This was ridiculous.

He'd have to go in, but how to save face? He couldn't just tell her the truth, that would be too hurtful. Also it would make him seem insane. He thought and thought, keeping his back to the house to protect at least one part of himself. A wind was picking up, and he was starting to feel dangerously chilled. What if he caught pneumonia?

Good manners would be the death of him. He would have to go somewhere, so he could walk back to his house from some distance, in case she was still looking. He'd say he'd gone for a walk earlier, not taken a jacket and forgotten the time. He'd pretend to be surprised, but he'd pretend to be worried first. Maybe he'd grab a big stick. He'd shout in a masterful voice: Who's there? Then she'd answer and he'd drop the stick and say: Why, it's only you!

*

He snuck further into his back garden, still hunched over, then through the hawthorn hedge. He was now scratched and slightly bleeding, as well as soaked to the skin. He stood up and began trotting through the field. It began to hail. The hailstones were big. They bounced off his bare head, cruelly reminding him he was bald now. He kept forgetting how old he was.

Something ran towards him, low and growling. The nameless stray dog that terrified all the children in the area, and most of the adults too. He growled at everyone, even people who took pity and threw him bones. He ran and ran, till he was nearly at the bottom of his track, the dog nipping his ankles anytime he slowed. One of his ankles felt like it was bleeding. Maybe he'd need a tetanus shot. How soon would he need to get one? Tonight? He felt his chest burn. His breath was rasping, almost a wheeze as if he was having an asthma attack. He wondered if he was, indeed, now asthmatic. He wished he could run faster, but he was overweight and he used to smoke. Oh yes, he'd forgotten that too. Bald and fat and wrecked lungs. And now bleeding, soaking wet, and possibly rabies-ridden. Imminent death loomed, but that was not a new feeling. *You're hypochondriac,* every single one of his girlfriends had said. What did they know?

Suddenly the dog gave up, barked twice in salutation and slunk away. After his panting slowed, he clambered over the barbed-wire fence on to his track. He was clumsy and his jeans tore on the barbs. He looked down and noticed they'd torn a huge flap from the pocket to the crotch, so no matter what he did to rearrange himself, the front of his underpants was visible, as well as part of his skinny thigh, also bleeding. Oh well, he thought – the tetanus shot for the dog bite would cover this too.

He was wearing underpants given to him by his mother, years ago. Greying, but you could still see the smiling green face of Shrek. Would it be better to take off his underpants and expose his genitals? Which was worse? Shrek or his penis? In the end, he took off his tee shirt, tucked it into his jeans waistband, so it hung like a miniskirt over Shrek.

*

As he walked towards his lit house, he could no longer feel his feet. Then he noticed it had stopped hailing. The dog had distracted him from this good news, but now he let himself appreciate the lack of exfoliating ice on his skin. And the rain was light now, with no wind at all. Delicious. Soon, a warmth spread through him. Perhaps he'd had a heart attack after all. If he was dying, by God he was going to enjoy every last drop of life. He opened his mouth and began singing the first song that popped into his head, which was 'Bring it on Home' by the Everly Brothers. He felt young suddenly, his chest bared like a kid, his belly swinging over his miniskirt tee shirt, his legs and arms swinging to beat the band. His feet made moist sucking sounds in his sodden shoes.

*

He looked ahead to his house and pictured her standing by the window watching him approach. Maybe she was smiling. Maybe she was even laughing a little, out of relief. Relief flooded him too. It was good to be coming home. Even with a woman inside, it was still good. And he felt grateful to her. If she'd not been so bold, this night would have slipped into obscurity like millions of others. But when he got to his front door, he felt shy. As if it was he who was the guest, not sure of his welcome. Or as if he was a ghost, looking through his own window at the life he'd had, or could have had.

Rose Ruane

THE GHOST AT HELLY'S WAKE

It's only when I turn off the motorway into the flat grey edgelands of the town that I realise just how much I don't want to be here.

I knew it as an abstract skeletal ache when I started the car at dawn, kicking my cramped feet out of my high heels, the only black shoes I could find in my half-woken stupor. I encountered it as a mild dyspepsia of the heart when I bought bad coffee under the aggressive fluorescent lights of a service station two hours ago. But only here, only now, as the blank warehouses of the industrial estate hulk on the margins of my vision do I connect intimately with my true resistance as recalled boredoms, old kinds of sadness made new, crowd painfully under my breastbone.

The sharp tug of repulsed nostalgia for the town of my youth makes me drive badly and I almost cause a crash on the junction by my old school as I crane to take in its sameness and difference. I pull over for a moment to let the giddy mixture of adrenaline and melancholy subside, staring at the squat unattractive building with an uncanny sense that I might see my young self moving behind its windows.

I recall acutely the well-worn tedium of lessons, thin notes of inexpertly played piano drifting down the long corridors while I gazed out across the playing fields, glad that I was not bare-legged and cloth-bibbed on the hockey pitch, longing for a shapeless, nameless, better life I had not yet begun to live. I pull away reluctantly, sorry for my teenage self with her hopes which will prove to be ill-founded, sorry for my adult self who holds the proof that that's the case.

I reach the cemetery gates and hum a few bars of the Smiths. The tune feels inappropriately jaunty on my lips and I let it tail off into cold whisper as the car creeps slowly past the old graves with their flock of moss and the newer ones, still tended by browning flowers with their curled cellophane wrappers fluttering in the wind.

As I pull into the car park by the chapel I see the shivering mourners huddled like rooks on a branch: waiting to test themselves against death. Helly's death. And as I let the engine stutter to a halt I wonder why I have come. Perhaps some morbid desire to try out grief, rehearse a future where funerals are more common than weddings and grief is not untimely or out of place, where all our hair will be grey, the interior of the crematorium familiar as a supermarket. The houses of death will be places we visit as a matter of course. I had not seen Helly for years. I cannot picture her the way she must have been when the Mercedes hit her bicycle, replacing Helly as a fact in the world with the sudden particulars of her death.

Denise greets me as I step out of the car. We wear our faces with a degree of embarrassment, inventorying changes; the stubborn lines of reproof which have settled permanently at the corner of a lip, the deep furrow between the brows which no longer shallows, however pleasant and open the current expression.

'Alice!' she says, pulling me into a loose embrace. 'You look great.' Then thinks better of the civil untruth: 'Isn't it awful?' she says, biting her lip in a way which strikes me as heartbreakingly familiar despite the shameful quantity of lapsed time in which we have not spoken.

'It is,' I say, trying out the right attitudes, the proper rhythms for the attendance of untimely death. 'I can hardly believe it.' Denise takes my arm and we walk towards the chapel that way, the way we always did; linked at the elbow conspiratorially.

The light has that crepuscular quality, bearing the hallmarks of both the beginning and end of the day despite it being early afternoon, and it seems mad to me that we are here, that we are old, older anyhow, that we are adults – our normal progress through life feels absurd. That we girls are mothers, teachers, GPs, lawyers, even though it seems to me that we should still be young, our lives untried. We shuffle into a pew next to Cara, who Helly, Denise and I were only ever sort of friends with. At the front of the church Helly's parents are crying with her husband while her small children look around, hushed by not understanding quite what is coming to pass.

'Poor little things,' says Cara. 'How are you?'

'Fine,' I say. 'Fine.' Not prepared for small talk, not prepared to explain how small the dimensions of my world are in comparison to the wide horizons I was facing down when last we met. Which was when? A languid summer's return home from university eighteen years ago? Probably: we used to meet when the gaps in the holiday which were once full of promise had filled up with tedium, still pleasantly surprised that we could rightfully go to the pub. We would pretend we were all still close while inside we strained to return to our new lives and be free of the discomfiting sojourn into the old ones we were in the process of outgrowing, comparing the intimates of our recently dispensed-with childhoods unfavourably with the friends we had made at university as our conversations turned bitchy and competitive.

'How are you?' I ask Cara, but before she can reply a familiar music starts up, something by Van Morrison, and Helly's coffin is borne in on the shoulders of her relatives. Her son shouts, 'Mummy,' a grieved exclamation from the depths of his small soul and then his sister starts to cry. It is almost impossible to bear: the children's noisily wounded bafflement that a long box topped with roses should mean their mother now. Denise and I hold hands tightly, transmitting a silent apology through our palms that we were so careless with the tender complicity of our youth.

The service is short; describing a woman I did not know who grew out of a girl with whom I was almost as familiar as I was with myself. And I recall meeting Helly in the evenings to lie on the flat roof of the bus shelter head to head, our bodies in an A-frame, smoking cigarettes she stole from her grandma's handbag on a Sunday afternoon. It suddenly seems ridiculous that we drifted apart so easily in the intervening years – letters I began and never completed, promises to meet which time proved to be meaningless, like a dropped line, a missed call, a broken connection which can never be remade. I begin to cry, a modest quantity of tears to denote that I understand that something which could have remained important did not and is lost. I should have danced at her wedding but I was backpacking round India with a man who broke my heart.

As the service ends we shuffle out, bruised into silence, dabbing at our puffy eyes. I am shocked when Denise lets go of my arm to speak to Helly's husband. I watch from the distance as she bends down kindly to offer soft comforts to the children, which they accept. The daughter puts her small arms round Denise's neck. I imagine how hot and damp and heavy the small body must be in Denise's arms as she lifts her up and I realise *they were still friends*. Without me. And I feel profoundly stupid: without reason I had assumed we had *all* drifted apart. Arrogantly, in the solipsistic way which has served me so badly all this time, I had thought that we were each of us dispersed, never considering that the old ties I had slipped from still kept the others delicately, willingly bound to one another. I suppose I must have thought I was the axis on which they all turned, that they would fly apart without my precious gravity to hold them in orbit of one another. Cara is there too, soothing the children, hugging Denise with the genuine tenderness of good friends. Bitterly I find myself thinking: But we were only ever sort of friends with Cara. I decide not to go to the wake and determine to slip away unnoticed as it seems I ever did.

In the vestibule Helly's parents are wanly shaking hands with the dispersing crowd. Inadvertently I catch her mother's eye and she says, 'Alice?'

Reluctantly I go to her and offer my inadequate condolences. I search her face for some rebuke but find none. She thanks me for coming, says it's such a shame that Helly and I drifted apart, says that Helly would have loved that I have come. I want to apologise to her for everything that's insufficient about me, to excuse the narcissism of the assumptions I never realised I had made, to express my regret that somewhere in the back of my mind I must have thought that there was a gap of my exact dimensions in this place where we grew up, not realising that life heals up quickly around absences, like the surface of a pond closes over the decreasing rings of a dropped stone. The words for these thoughts constrict my throat and I say nothing. I simply squeeze one of Helly's mother's small cold hands in my larger warmer one with all the kind intent I can muster and veer away, surprised to find that the sun is out and that rain is falling from an impossibly blue sky.

I fumble for my car keys, selfish tears bulging in the corners of my eyes, and I am ashamed that I am not crying for Helly or her children but for myself, for everything that has failed, for all the good that the version of myself which was last in this place believed was coming and which never did. As I open the car door, Denise and Cara appear and ask for a lift to Helly's wake. Feeling a heel, but full of my own injured need to leave, I tell them I can't stay. 'Well that's typical,' huffs Cara, 'I don't know why I'm surprised.'

Denise reprimands her with a glare, and I could hug her for the undeserved loyalty, then I see a look pass between them, a barely perceptible roll of the eyes which says, Of course. Of course Alice isn't going to the wake. My selfish resolve evaporates into the mutability I always loathed in myself and I truculently invite them to get in. Feeling humiliated I start the engine and immediately stall the car. I put my head on the steering wheel and start to howl like an infant. I feel the trapped air of the car shift as Denise and Cara exchange a look. Denise puts her hand on my back, kindly, gently, then from the back seat Cara says, 'For fuck's sake. It always had to be all about you, didn't it?'

'She's just overwhelmed,' says Denise, but her tone belies an irritated ennui which shames me. It says, This is what Alice is like, this is what Alice was always like.

'Don't make excuses for her,' snaps Cara. 'She hadn't seen Helly for years, she never even cared how hurt Helly was.' I marshal myself, dry my eyes, and still sobbing start the car. Cara says sorry and I tell her it's fine and then no one says anything else until we reach the hotel where the wake is being held.

We get out of the car. Cara and Denise walk ahead of me, complicit in something silently decided during the car journey, and some old shame is on me like a wet coat. It tumbles over in my gut like ungraspable déjà vu and I take a deep breath before I go inside.

Cara and Denise are with Helly's husband. I cannot help but notice that they seem bilious with an excessive awareness of how *good* they are being, how certain they are of the wise and kind nature of the aphoristic comforts they offer to him, how spectacularly they know they have risen to meet the profound demands of this previously untried horror. Then I am ashamed – maybe this is just apposite kindness between friends and I am sour from the unpleasantness in the car.

'Alice,' says Denise, 'this is Alan; Helly's husband.'

I shuffle closer. 'I'm sorry,' I say, my words coming from a place far inside me, reaching the air as an idiocy which inflates into a miasma I can almost see. The guests bustle round the buffet table, floppy paper plates quivering with beige food.

Alan shakes my hand. 'The famous Alice, thank you for coming.' There is something wry, almost mocking in his tone. 'Helly often talked about you.'

'I can't imagine why,' I say, then feel chastened by the self-pitying baldness of the statement. I stare at the shoes which are pinching my toes maddeningly and wonder why I can't connect with any of this;

finding it easier to throw my whole being into podiatric discomfort than to live this moment with any wholeness.

'Hey,' says Alan, his hand on the cuff of my coat, 'I'm sure you both always thought you'd reconnect – I think Helly always thought you would one day.'

I see he is a kind man who was probably not mocking me earlier. I see Cara and Denise whispering like witches, damning me for forcing this gesture of conciliation from a freshly widowed man. 'Time,' I say.

And Alan knows what I mean. 'Yes,' he says, 'I suppose we always think there will be time.' The poor man is being good about this for both of us, for three of us.

'Helly used to love telling me about your seances. She told me about the haunted house.' He smiles, slipping from the moment into a reverie of he and Helly, the sort of talking about the past as people do in bed when night makes them fear how far they have come from themselves and makes them want to reach for memories of uncomplicated times.

'We were morbid little things,' I say, then someone coughs at my elbow and I make way for them to give Alan their condolences. I hope theirs are more adeptly offered than mine.

I shuffle awkwardly through the crowded room towards Denise and Cara. 'He seems nice,' I say. As if we were all still schoolgirl confidantes, as if he and Helly had just met. Cara rolls her eyes and I attempt to be better than I feel. 'He said Helly told him about the seances, about the haunted house.'

'God,' says Denise, looking disgusted. 'What a weird thing to bring up.' This lands on me as an accusation.

'I was never invited to your freaky occult stuff,' says Cara bitterly.

Denise rubs her arm. 'It was all silly stuff, Alice was so dramatic. No one believed in it except her,' she says.

I smile wanly, but my heart hurts because Helly and I believed, or at least we wanted to. We wanted to conjure some dark magic into the bland security of our quiet suburb where nothing, maddeningly, continued to happen. Helly and I were bound by the hope that we could invoke some transcendent power which would be proof that the turgid routines of long days waiting to live were not all we might expect: we ached at the universe, tugging at the pockets of maybe which we hoped would unload all wonder into the dullness of our teenage lives.

Cara's mouth goes pouchy chewing on a sausage roll and I remember then why we never invited her to join our fruitless, half-honest, half-nonsense attempts at witchcraft.

'You broke into that house,' says Cara, little flecks of mashed-up sausage roll exposed on her tongue. Denise smiles and then suppresses it from deference to Cara.

'The haunted house?' I say. 'We climbed in through an open window.'

'God, I was so scared!' exclaims Denise. I can see that against her will she is swayed by the potency of the memory. The house was on Denise's street. She lived in a more affluent area than Helly and I, who came from the bungalows near the school. Every day there were workmen at the empty house, then one day they never came back and we, with our painful hunger for a mystery, convinced ourselves that the house was haunted, that the workmen had fled in terror of their lives. Then one day, when summer holiday tedium had maddened our appetites for something, anything, we could believe was special, we decided to investigate.

'Scooby Doo,' says Cara, sarcastically, between bites of an unappealing sandwich.

'That's just what we were like!' says Denise and they feast on the joke between them, not a crumb of amusement in it for me while I remember how deliciously we thrummed with fear as we climbed through the open window of the house, partly terrified we would be caught by an adult, partly terrified that the ghost we only believed in a little would show itself to us in the darkness.

'There was a ghost though, wasn't there, Alice?' says Denise slyly. She jabs Cara in the ribs with her elbow as if to say 'This will be good', and I wonder how I mistook our hand-holding at the funeral for anything more meaningful than a courteous reflex in a moment of dire confusion. I remember moving through the damp air of that abandoned house, Helly, Denise and I, savouring the confection of our fear. Then, as the tension reached its apex, Helly let go a banshee wail and pushed me over. Denise straddled my chest and delivered a series of stinging slaps to my face. She laughed between shouts of 'It's a ghost! It's a ghost!' Then they ran from the empty house, leaving me in tears, blinking around at the open pots of paint while dustsheets stirred in the breeze from the open window.

'No,' I say to Denise. 'There wasn't a ghost. The house wasn't haunted. Then as now we were in recession – the people renovating the house must have run out of money.' And I recall that moment in the afterward, stewing in the memory of Denise and Helly's laughter at my expense, and I see now that that was when the fracture between us began. It stopped being Helly and me and started being Helly and Denise. Helly and Denise against me.

I rise to leave, saying nothing, thinking, Fuck them, thinking childhood friendships are maybe only ever an expedient reaching out to those most like, or those least *unlike* yourself in a period where your world is redrawn thousands of times a day by obscure and absolute forces beyond your control. Thinking I never really believed in ghosts and seances and haunted houses – those were only games to fill the holes in me which boredom and an unappeasable want for something too big and far away to name were always opening up.

'Where are you going?' asks Denise. And I don't say anything, I just go. I remember now why I let those friendships slide so easily: after the haunted house, it seemed as if Helly and Denise always needed me to laugh at. Mocking my obdurate strangeness was what alleviated the tedium of their adolescence and all the hurts and humiliations of that time burn in me like the righteous anger I could never afford before. They only ever played along with my mystical fancies so they could find sameness together in my difference and share their laughter at my expense like tuck-shop goodies after midnight.

I climb into the car and point myself towards home, which is far from here and contains little of what my young self hoped for, yet I am glad to be returning there or at least glad to be leaving here.

As I pull away from the hotel, a thin mist is collecting on the surface of the fields, beginning to erase the details of this place at once familiar to me yet so changed. Some restive worry which twists in me has been settled by this; sampling the anger I always denied myself has soothed me somehow. I think of holding hands with Helly at a seance, of candles guttering in the wind as I called upon the spirits to reveal themselves while she and Denise shook with laughter. Of Ouija boards which spelled out my death every time but never foresaw Helly's bicycle being hit by a Mercedes when she was only thirty-six. And I am sorry she is dead, but not sorry that we failed to stay friends, if that is what we ever were, as mist obscures the edgelands of the town like a dirty thumbprint on glass.

Stewart Sanderson

ABSENTEES

Theirs is a shadowy luxuriance,
these spirits, who are like ourselves in all
but one particular. They lack presence.
Their grossness is unverifiable
and trembles at the limit of each sense
as a conceit; a metaphysical
contortion of improbability
between the conscious and reality.

They are the relatives we never met
who share our furniture and silverware:
an old loss which our grandchildren inherit
with death duties, freckles, thinning hair
whether or not they are aware of it.
They crowd around us, trapped in some elsewhere
the other side of memory: a room
exactly like this in another time.

They are the former owners of our homes
who seem to pass us in the corridor
between bathroom and kitchenette, but whom
we never see. Behind the bedroom door
they wait, eternally, for us to come
forwards into their arms. Theirs is the power
of pure potential: lustral silences
shattered by our unwitting entrances.

Sometimes, they are intruders whom we know
by absent bodies other than their own:
the vanished laptop or the stolen glow
of jewellery. Often, they are the one –

the ones, even – whose absence does not show
in misplaced concrete things. Try to imagine,
say, your childhood sweetheart and the wife
she never was. This is to test belief.

This is credulity. Imagine them
who are no different from ourselves, except
they never were. Consider her, then him
who is a version of the boy who slipped
away one ancient day. You share a name
and everything which neither could escape:
a common root from which your difference grows;
ancestral whispers in the tangled shadows

of your lives. Open your heart to these
which are mere variations on yourself:
your amplitude; your possibilities
spending themselves into an endless gulf
of roads untook. I call them absentees
as you will be one day, who own your skelf
of presence for a time. Try to remember
them, who are unreal, and without number.

Andrew Sclater

NURSERY RHYME

Don't talk to Mother, she is feeding your brother.
Don't talk to Mother, or else she will smother you.
Don't talk to Father, either. You are NOT to bother
Father – he is at work. Run along. Stop lurking. Now DO
what I say. And DON'T answer back. Put on your shoe.
There are places I know for children like you …
Stop making faces. Get out.
Do up your laces. Wipe your snout.

Shelley Day Sclater

THE MEMORY BOX

The words my mother said, I kept them, I made a list, I added to it daily. At first just singletons, a few small phrases. Then things, I listed things, the things she hoarded: mostly toys, her brother's, broken. I crammed everything into the box that used to be for fuse wire, tacks, screws, nails. I fixed a metal clasp on and jammed the lid shut, just in time. There was a lot of noise: my mother's voice, and all the other stuff clamouring, hammering, yammering, bashing at the sides. And that box rocking about like a jumping bean.

For safe keeping, I left the box on a shelf with a big stone on top.

Every now and then I'd have a little look, a little listen. I might detect a low-level electrical hum – that had to be the new Kelvinator, 1962. Or water moving – the river at the foot of Ben Nevis, the way it rushes down the glen after the melt, swirling copper-brown round the feet of the alders. Or there'd be a sticky sweet almost sickly smell – candy floss from the Hoppings; tastes nice but rots your teeth.

*

The box had been quiet for several weeks. I was looking at it sitting there on the shelf with its stone on top and before I knew what I was doing, I had lifted the stone off, laid it to one side and I was standing there, expecting something to happen. Nothing did. There was no movement, no noise. The box was docile. So I undid the clasp. I opened the lid a fraction. I put my ear to the opening. It was quiet and still. So I allowed myself just the tiniest, the quickest wee peek.

No sooner had my squinting eye drawn level with the slit of an opening than I was overwhelmed with a sensation, a peculiar sensation I've not known, before or since, which makes it difficult to describe. It was like longing but it was not longing. It caused my insides to flinch and to stay flinched. It was like a yearning that had no object or reason or purpose. It was wet and raw and stripped of civilisation.

The frantic buzzing of a bluebottle caught in the cobwebbed skylight of my attic pulled me back from the strange place to which the box had taken me. My only thought was to clamp the lid back on. I don't know how long that took, the trapped creatures fought me all the way, hissing and snapping, cajoling and pleading, snarling abuse. Finally I got the clasp done up. I sank back exhausted, while in front of me on the floor the box jostled and jumped and cursed all manner of vile accusations. The next hours I spent fitting a second, stronger, clasp. And then I put on a third, on a metal band, which took me well into the small hours.

A solid dreamless sleep and I woke to the knowledge of Things crawling over me. I could feel them on the bed, under the covers, jostling around my head on the pillow. I leapt up, afraid that at any moment I'd be suffocated.

Immediately I saw it – the lid of the box was flung open, its clasps wrenched apart, its hinges twisted. The box was tipped over on its side, empty. Its contents swarmed about the room, squelching and cackling. The whole place stinking of herring guts and creosote and ironing, mothballs, liver and onions, perm lotion and Elizabeth Arden Blue Grass. In my mouth I could taste those thick brown drops my mother always took to help her manage. The old toys of her brother's she'd clung on to all those years – tinny wind-up things – they were clicking and marching and tumbling on their sides, whirring staccato and rusty through their paces. Dolls with cracked ceramic faces and stained cloth bodies lay slumped in piles, their blank eyes staring, their legs and arms at all angles. But worst of all were my mother's words. They were crawling round over everything, millions of wiry little specimens speeding up and down the walls, scuttling in and out of everywhere, hissing and cursing. Vehemence spattered the walls, piles of disappointment congealed in corners, envy oozed into the woodwork, clagging up the door frame, dripping through the floor.

*

Clara says why not write a letter to your mother. Put in all the words you could never say to her.

Okay, I say, but then I get stuck on the first line. What am I supposed to put after the 'Dear'? I can't force any of the usual words out, I just cannot.

Ah, says Clara, let's take it from there.

Clara is a strange fish. She wears odd shoes, different colours, one red, one green. She sits on the floor, under the window where the light is such I can't make out her face. In its place is a darkness, a silhouette, with wild curly hair. Clara's legs, in crumpled linen trousers, are hugged up against her chest so the shoes point across the room towards me, openly declaring their distance and their difference. I am conscious of my own feet facing hers across the no man's land of the stripped-pine floor.

I buy some strappy fuck-me shoes that I can hardly walk in and I team them up with the short black PVC coat, genuine retro – I'm old enough to own the real McCoy. I pull the belt tight French-style and tie a knot. I put the dark glasses on. It's difficult getting up Clara's stairs with the shoes and the glasses on, but I manage.

What d'you think you're playing at? Who the hell do you think you are?

Clara stares at my shoes, plus I've left the coat on and I'm sitting on the chair instead of lying on the couch.

You're spineless. No backbone. Touched, that's what you are. You need your head examined.

We sit for a little while in silence. The fact that I am paying dear for this makes me the first person to speak.

I couldn't write to my mother, I say, but I put all her words in a box.

There she goes again, making her mag go, mouth like Tynemouth. I'll give her something to whine about.

In a box, says Clara.

Yes, a box, I say. But they've burst the lid off and they've all got out. They've taken over my life, I mean my attic. It's a question of how to get them all back in. Into the box.

Tell-tale-tit, tongue shall be slit, and all the little dicky birds ... Knock your teeth down your throat, that's what I'll do.

On the wall to the right of me is a picture of the sea looking wild and unpredictable, you can almost hear it hollering. Behind the couch is a smaller one, a painting of a harbour, little coloured boats at all unlikely angles, like they're about to tip out of the canvas.

Do you want to go on the couch, Clara asks when she sees me looking over there.

I'll murder you. I'll swing for you. Nasty little liar. Get out of my sight.

The blue and white boat in the foreground is called *Our Girls*. It's been pulled up out of the sea and is stranded on the pebbly shore beside a road.

No, I've told you, I say. I take my coat off, lay it over my knees, hold on to it.

This is my mother's cardigan, I say. She knitted it.

Don't you dare touch anything of mine. Keep your filthy hands out.

She made it for you, says Clara.

No, she made it for herself.

But you're wearing it, says Clara. I thought you gave her clothes to Oxfam.

I did, but I kept some.

It's hard to say goodbye to her, says Clara.

I curse the day you were born. I'll be glad to see the back of you.

She's been dead three years, I say.

All the same, says Clara, pushing her legs out straight and rubbing her knees.

There's an enormous bunch of white lilies on a tall table in the corner by the window near where Clara sits. Their scent is strong; I smell it over here. They are wide open. There are always fresh flowers in Clara's room. And little piles of smooth stones. Like eggs.

Lilies, for purity, I say.

What do you want to wear your mother's clothes for, asks Clara.

How d'you think I might get those words back in the box, I ask Clara.

You could start by putting the clothes in, Clara says.

*

She wants to strip me naked, so I'll oblige.

Give me a box, I say, I'll put them in, here and now.

I start pulling the clothes off and soon I'm starkers, except for the shoes still on. Clara is impassive and I'm stood there, naked. I sit back down. The fifty minutes will soon be up, and what will she say then. Will she let me flounce down the stairs in only the shoes? Stumble down her street with nothing on?

Clara chances a glance at the little clock she keeps near her.

How does it feel, to be so exposed, she asks.

You promised me a box, I say, but you've let me down, you've let me down, you always let me down.

I'm on your side, she says.

Is this a game of ping-pong, I ask.

Ping-pong, Clara says, as though it is a question.

Ping-pong, I say, in the manner of a statement.

*

Clara and I are looking at each other's shoes.

You're wearing odd shoes, I say.

Yours are a little odd too, says Clara.

Odd, I say, with the question inflection.

Yes, says Clara, yes. She glances at the clock again.

The box, I say, I need the box. I'm all out in goosebumps. I could just about be sick.

Your mother's dead, Clara says. You've buried her.

Yes, I put her in a box and I buried her.

Clara gets up and hands me a tartan blanket.

You can let her go, she says.

*

I put my things back on, everything except the cardigan. As I turn to go, I bundle the cardigan under the seat, take a last look at the painting of the harbour. All the little coloured boats, all so safely moored, *Our Girls* pulled up there, on the pebbles, by the road.

David Scott

THE SIXTH OF DECEMBER

The house is wrapped up tight
in its coat of rain. I put their pyjamas
under their pillows. The furry blankets rise
and fall and swell like organ music –

all of his birthday cards and books and pipe cleaners –
lost in the wind.

An exhibit in a museum 'A Cornish Coastal Path'.
Put it in a glass case
five miles long. A box for
everything. Ash on the wet black stones.

In the black car up to the cemetery
I saw the soft wind
shake the yew trees
and the psalms broke over us

like giant waves of Cornwall
breaking themselves over footprints and giant rocks.

*

Anything could be an exhibit
in a one-man show. A tennis court
scratched in the sand. A life in
parcels. My small pail in his big hand

going over to set free the crabs
which had always
crawled off in the morning.
Those young hands round a rifle
or my mother's hair.

*

The sixth of December
is a good day if somewhat damp, with
the wind turned around to the east
and the brand new foghorn blowing

just now and again. It is a warm
wind strangely. But then we are much
further south. His dressing gown is
hanging on my bedroom

door where I left it this morning
and went down to tell the boys
they were late for school.

Nancy Somerville

LOVER'S SON

I saw him on the bus today,
a younger version of you.
It was the voice that drew me in
and the way he laughed,
one hand holding the phone to his ear
(I could tell it was a woman)
the other tapping a rhythm on the seat,
and his hair, black and fine
as my fingers remembered,
the Kirk Douglas chin I teased you about
and the way he sat, that easy confidence.

As I passed to go downstairs
he sneezed. 'Bless you,' I said
and he gave me your smile.

Dan Spencer

STREAM

Claire comes in. She says, Good morning, it's Claire. Having a lie-in? She says, Here we are. Up we get. Her outfit is blue. Her bare arms slip under my arms. She says, Am I your first visitor? and I say I was speaking to Peter. She says, What sort of day is it? then, What a day. Look at this day. A busy day today. She's right. Just look. It's a bright day. Bright gravel outside. Bright grass. A fair amount of trees. Just look at that sun.

Sue comes in. She says, Richard says hi. Richard sends his love. He sends his apologies, but he has a lot on. He couldn't get away. She says, How am I? How am I feeling today? I look well today, she says. Have I eaten? Did they bring breakfast? Have they been in? Her skirt is white and orange and pink. She could be seventeen, in that white and orange and pink skirt. She says Kate is coming later with Luke. She says Emma might be coming later with Nicholas. Remember Nicholas?

Kate comes in. She sits in a chair. She pulls a chair up close. She says, Are you having a good day today, a special sort of day? I'm glad we could come, she says. We didn't know we could come. We're a good distance away now, remember? It's a good flat we've got. Luke has a job. Luke's good.

And I notice that a boy is standing behind her. He's awkward and handsome. He's standing at the window. It's a big, bright window but he's shadowy. Hello Peter, I say. How are you? and Kate says, No, this is Luke, remember? And that makes me look back at her. It's a beautiful face the girl has. Her hair is cut close to the head. Who does she remind me of? She's a beautiful girl, this girl I'm looking at. I'm smiling at her then Sue says, It's Kate, Mum. It's your granddaughter Kate.

Betty visits. Betty comes to the door. She's an untidy child. She says am I in? She says can I come out? My mother says out with the both of you, out. Look at that day, says my mother. Children should be out in it. Children should be out, not in. She's wearing a yellow dress, my mother. The sleeves are pushed up to the elbow. Her bare arms lift me outside. Back by dinnertime, she says. Not before then. Out you go. Out with you. Out, out.

Emma visits. Emma says, I know that I could visit more. It isn't possible. I never have an hour free. You know that I'm responsible for all recruitment now? And all of London and the South of England. Michael says I do too much for them, she says. Michael says I should up and quit. He says I should get myself headhunted, she says. Yes, I say, yes. A lovely couple. You two always were a lovely couple, I say. Thank you, says Emma but Sue says, You haven't met Michael, Mum. It's Nicholas you're thinking of. It's Nicholas you've met. Then I say, We were saying what a lovely couple you two always were. I was saying it to Peter ... No, says Emma. You weren't saying it to Peter, Gran, and Sue says, Emma, don't, she knows, she does know that, she knows ...

A cat comes in. They have a cat here. I forgot the cat. It's entirely black, walking around on the carpet. It jumps on to the bed. Hello, I say. What's your name? Henrietta comes in. Henrietta says, Who are you? What are you doing in here? She says, This is my room. Get out! Henrietta is a madwoman. Then Claire comes and says Sorry and, Come on Hen. The baby comes in. He totters about. He's only just walking. He's having a glorious time, with his walking. His mother comes in. She says, Bert! Not in there. This way, Bert. Come away. Bertie. Bert! Then the young man re-enters. He's sullen and handsome. He's shadowy. He says, What happened? Where is everyone? Have they left? I should go. Well, goodbye.

The prime minister's wife. She's wearing an emerald dress. She sits on the bed. She puts both her hands on my knees. She says, It's a pleasure to meet you, and who are you? And how are they treating you? How are you keeping? She's wearing a purple and indigo dress. You can't expect too much, she says. You do what you can and that's all. What matters is can you look back and be happy? Her dress is a red dress. It's really too red. Then the cat is outside. We watch it walk by at the window, both of us, pausing, this woman and me. And there are trees here and there. Big trees. A generous amount of trees. The gravel is bright. The cat is a very bright grey.

My grandmother visits. She enters the room, with great effort. She sits in her chair. My mother, bare-armed, attends to her. What does she need? She doesn't need anything. She wants for nothing. She doesn't say a word. I watch her. What is her Christian name? What is her maiden name? What a mystery she is. I don't know if she sees me? She's staring at nothing. She seems to be watching somebody somewhere. She looks very old. She looks close to death. She is dressed all in black from her neck to her ankles. She is sixty-five.

I remember the day that Richard was born. A long labour. I was all in my body. I wasn't in my head at all. I couldn't think. I remember, I couldn't think anything, including I couldn't think what I was there for. I couldn't remember my own name or the day of the week. Then they lifted up Richard. They put Richard in my arms and I looked at him, surprised. I knew that I knew him from somewhere but I couldn't remember from where. I said to him, Oh, so it's you. There you are.

When I tell that to Peter he says, If that is the happiest day of your life, shall I tell you the happiest day of my life? I say yes and he says, It's the day I decided to marry you. You old romantic, I say. You old boy. Then he talks and I listen as he's talking. I could listen to him talk all day. He could talk the sun into the sky, the old rogue. I'm listening. It's getting late. They've all gone home. It's dusk, I think, by the look of it.

Peter says, Do you remember? You were working in town. I was on nights that day. You were finishing at five o'clock and going straight home to your parents' house. We weren't going to meet. We hadn't known each other for long, at this point. You wouldn't call it love, at this point. But I was awake and with nothing to do. I mean I couldn't think of anything to do, so I decided to visit you, I decided to come and meet you. It was all I wanted to do, I mean, so I walked into town.

I didn't hurry. I took my time. It was a summer's day. It was bright. As I walked, I looked at all the people passing by. Some faces I knew and some I didn't. A lot of different heads, bobbing by in the sunshine. They were like a lot of different objects – everyday objects, household objects – bobbing past you on a river. Imagine that – a walk beside a little river, and all these things bobbing past you on the current – a clock, saucepans, a telephone …

I looked at all these people moving on the street and I realised that at any moment you'd appear, at any moment one of them would turn out to be you. So, I was walking along and looking around and looking forward to the moment when we'd meet. It would be like the sun coming out on an already really very sunny day. It was good, walking like that, expecting you at any moment. But that wasn't the incredible thing.

Then, as I was walking, I noticed a girl coming towards me from a distance. For a moment you were a stranger I liked the look of. I liked you in your shop uniform, in your blouse and your big pleated skirt. Then I saw you. I saw it was you. That was good, too, recognising you, I mean seeing someone I liked then seeing it was you. But it wasn't the incredible thing, either.

Then I saw you see me. I saw you recognise that it was me. And you smiled about it. And it was incredible. That was the moment. That was the incredible thing. I was yours from then on. I'll never forget it. I saw my own name come into your head. All of a sudden. Out of nowhere.

Peter.

Pop!

Alison Summers

THE DEPARTMENT FOR RECYCLED MEN

The plague that swept through the computer industry damaged all of its employees but men were particularly badly affected. When I first started work in the Department for Recycled Men, I used to process about twenty donations per week but after the plague, the numbers increased so much I had to employ two assistants. The work isn't arduous, just time-consuming and you must have an eye for detail. In pre-plague days, customers were less fussy. They would hand over their donation and say things like 'Would you just check to see if he's still alive? He hasn't said anything for weeks.' Occasionally they just sent a donation in for a bit of rehab. If we weren't able to separate the donation from his mobile phone by the end of the week, a customer would usually let us keep him and we sent him to charity. The charities were ruthless. They used our addict donations for spare parts so it was always a hard decision.

I take a great pride in my work. At the end of a day there are few things more rewarding than a room full of recycled men. No day is ever the same. You wouldn't believe the variety we get here. Of course sometimes people abuse the system. I've had people turning up with bag ladies and tramps, pretending they found them slumped at their computer desk in the office. It's the reward system that makes things difficult. When plague-infected workers have no family or friends (more common than you might think) the government gives a small cash bonus to the person who donates them to us. It keeps the recycling flow regular and can add up to a nice little earner in large cities. But I can't do anything with a bag lady or a tramp. They just don't fit into the system.

The best donations come in to us a wee bit stunned and usually non-verbal. The first thing that happens is we pop them under the power shower for about ten minutes. Then, depending on what the customer has asked for, we give them a haircut, a waxing if needed, and my assistant sorts out some new clothes for them. I've seen men who've come in with beige cords six inches above their ankles, a harlequin tanktop over a green and brown striped polo shirt and sandals

with ribbed grey socks transformed by the application of proper fitting
jeans, white shirt, black socks, loafers and a nice leather jacket. Obviously
we can't do much about the body that's donated but it's fascinating
watching the donation's posture and facial expression change when they
see their new coverings. That's all just cosmetic though. The recycling
begins in earnest in the basement. It's soundproofed down there.

We work on re-establishing eye contact first. They're terribly shy at
first but once they understand what we ask of them, it only takes a bit
of practice and we're exchanging looks like there's no tomorrow. Takes
a bit longer to teach them opening gambits though. Especially since
they are used to having a screen in front of them for cues. Poor things,
some of them get panic attacks. You can see them searching the basement
for electric sockets, desks, wires, anything that might lead to a computer,
iPad or mobile phone's whereabouts. There's nothing to find. All our
records are compiled in a separate building. So no infections ever get
through to our treatment rooms. After a period of cold turkey they
stop fidgeting and eye-rolling and listen to what I'm saying.

'You've been brought here for recycling. Your wife/daughter/girlfriend/
colleague want only the best for you. No harm will come to you if you
just relax and enjoy the process.'

There's very seldom any aggression. Years of sublimating their testos-
terone reactions with computer games have numbed their fight or flight
responses. Occasionally I have to deal with the odd one or two who
have their own ideas about what they would like to be recycled into;
say an astronaut or a deep-sea diver. I have to make it clear that this
service is customer-driven. They get a bit huffy after that but eventually
they come round. After all, none of our customers want anything but
the best for the men they donate. They want the men to come home
as reasonable, functioning human beings. And useful. Of some use. So
no, it's no good begging me to make you into an Olympic bobsleigher
when your wife has specified she'd like someone who will take her to
the opera and converse nicely with her relatives at Christmas.

When I employed my assistants I warned them of the dangers of
becoming over-involved with the men. We do work so closely with
them that it's not surprising we react a wee bit emotionally when after
a hard day in the basement someone who presented as a catatonic
non-verbal gives us a hug and tells us we have nice hair. But these men

are spoken for. We are only processors. It is tricky when someone you
know is donated. The official guidelines say you should refuse to process
them and should hand them on to a colleague. One time I was looking
through the donations and recognised a name. Bill Henderson. I checked
to see who had brought him in and what kind of recycling they had
ordered. His colleague at British Gas had found him wandering up
and down a street punching numbers randomly into his tablet. He was
supposed to be taking meter readings but the plague had taken over
and he was out of control. At least he was found in the open air. God
knows what might have happened if an unsuspecting customer had
let him into her flat.

The last time I had seen Bill was at the school leaving ball. He was
excited about going off for his gap year in South America. Six months
helping to build an orphanage and then six months exploring and
painting. 'When I come back, Helen, I'll have a huge exhibition.'

And now here he was twenty years later. Sunburned, unshaven and
in anorak and ancient jeans, he looked like a tramp but his colleague
had assured me he was a bona fide employee of British Gas and had
shown me the paperwork. We started the process. It was only when
we got to the eye contact part that Bill recognised me. Yes, I know I
should have handed him over to someone else but my curiosity – well,
you'd have done the same I'm sure. We had unfinished business, Bill
and I. Also, when I saw what was written as 'preferred outcome' on the
application form I couldn't bear it.

'I never thought I'd see you again,' Bill croaked.

Plague victims' voices take a while to regain their normal level.

'Nor I you,' I said, trying very hard to keep my voice steady. Now
that he had been cleaned up and dressed in a suit, he was just as
attractive as he had been when twenty years ago he had kissed me in
the art room supplies cupboard.

Bill raked his newly manicured hands through his short dark hair.
'I tried to find you but they said you'd moved.'

I raised my eyebrow. 'Two years I waited to hear from you.'

'It was impossible to get a message out during the revolution. I was
locked up along with the rebels. I escaped when someone set the jail
on fire. It took weeks to find my way to a city with an embassy. All I
could think of was coming home to you. And then you weren't there.'

My heart was thumping like a sixteen-year-old's. 'What happened to your art?'

Bill shook his head. 'I'm no good.'

I couldn't bear to see him so dejected. 'I can recycle you differently if you want. You can try again. That's the whole point about recycling. Making something successful out of a failure.'

For a second I could see that Bill was considering it. Then he slumped in his chair as though someone had let all the air out of him. 'No, there's no point. Just do what you have to do.'

What choice did I have? Would you not do the same if your loved one looked like that?

I told the man from British Gas that the process had been unsuccessful. He signed the release forms and I took Bill to the room for charity donations. Just as I was about to leave him there, he took my hand and stroked my cheek. 'You've still got such nice hair,' he said. So I fixed the paperwork, smuggled him out and enrolled him in an adult education class: 'Art for the Terrified'. He's doing so well they are thinking of employing him as a tutor soon. Me? I've just won an award: Public Service Recycler of the year.

David Tallach

FOR EVA AND NINA

George Square that night,
Waiting for the wheel to turn
Centuries forward

Two girls and the flag,
Blue-cheeked as Boudiccas both
In their uprising

Soft-crumpling saltire
Told its own story, the folds
Shrouding the result

Thank you for standing,
Being our standard bearers
A night and a day

History is free
To more than just the winners,
The ones in the now

So lift up your heads,
You will enter your birthright:
We will dance again

Karen Thirkell

HOMER

'Can I haud ane?' she begs. 'Go on, gie's a shot.'

'Ye ken how much these are worth, lass?' Billy pauses at the doocot. In his grimy shovel hands, ingrained with pit dust, he holds a speckled bird.

'Aye, but I just want a shot. I'm still takin' them the day, amn't I?'

'If your faither says so. I hae ma doots. Ye're ower wee yet.'

'I'm nearly twelve!' Chrissie stands shivering in the dawn, her pinched face alight with excitement. The first hint of the sun can be glimpsed over the rooftops at the end of the miners' row but it will be some hours before it offers any warmth to the tiny yards at the back.

Billy sighs. Chrissie kens he thinks she's wee for her age but she's strong enough. He's seen her caw the mangle on wash day, if she reaches up on her tiptoes to push the handle to the top of its turn, she can force it back down on its arc, using all her weight. She may be wee richt enough but she's no feart o' hard work. But Billy would still take the doos himself if it wasn't so much cheaper for her ticket.

'Haud yer hands oot then, careful mind.' He speaks very softly so as not to startle the bird, and places it in Chrissie's outstretched hands. It is much lighter than she had expected. The downy soft feathers barely register on her calloused fingers and the doo's heartbeat flutters against the palm of her hand. She knows to hold it tightly enough so that it won't try to flap its wings but gently enough not to frighten or hurt it. She has watched her father and Billy many times but every request to have a shot of holding one of the prize birds has been rebuffed, until now. She strokes her thumb against the back of its neck, admiring the dark ring of feathers around the collar and the brown speckles on its wings like the splatters of mud on the backs of her school stockings.

'She's cried Anster Lass, eh, Uncle Billy? Worth a mint, Da said.' She holds the bird close to her chest, tilting it back towards her so that Billy can attach the metal tag to the ring on its leg. When the bird returns, the tag will be placed in the clock to be time-stamped.

'He's richt there.' Billy gives a swift smile. 'She better win some o' it back the day or I d'ae ken whaur she'll be next week.' He turns back to the doocot and lifts a sleek, black bird with bright orange eyes. He kisses the back of its head, deftly tags its leg and pops it in the basket.

'D'ae worry, she'll win. I'll mak shair.' Chrissie knows that Billy has taken a special interest in Anster Lass, she has seen him out at the doocot late in the evenings, talking to the bird and checking its beak, eyes, legs and wings with intense care. He fans each wing out, examining every feather, smoothing them down and all the time chattering softly in response to the bird's coos. He has even taken on the feeding, insisting to her Da that it needs a particular kind of corn he has managed to acquire through contacts – 'Dinnae ask me an' I'll no hae tae lee.'

*

'Ye'll manage twa baskets? That's fower doos and they'll a' need tae come oot at once on the whistle.' Da uses the stern voice that Chrissie recognises from his weekly instructions to her mammy to make the most of the housekeeping money, which does not 'faw fae the sky an is no to be pished doon the drain'. Chrissie nods with a vigour that threatens to dislodge her hat.

'I can manage, Da.'

'Well, mind ye dae, lass. It's nae use them finding their way back if they dinnae dae it afore the rest!' She sees his worn face – pitted as a moonscape, its lines permanently etched in coal dust – soften a little as he looks at her. 'Ach, yir lookin awfy like yir mither, lass. Let's see if ye've got her sense as weel as her curly hair.' He hands her the train fare with a further stern imprecation about keeping it safe.

'I'll gie ye a tanner when we win,' says Billy with a wink. 'Noo get a move on or ye'll miss the train.'

Already spending the tanner in her mind, Chrissie sets off down the street, the weight of the wicker baskets well distributed but barely clearing the ground as she swings them at her sides. It is half a mile down to the station in Leven and she is heading to Dunkeld for the release at midday. One hour to wait at the station there and then back home before seven. She has her piece in her pocket and Mammy has slipped her tuppence for a bottle of lemonade. The sun is shining and she feels it begin to warm her shoulders through the wool of her jumper. There is a hint of summer in the crisp stillness of the morning but, just off the shore, she can see a bank of haar building up on the Forth. She wonders if she will see anything much from the train. She is eager for the sight of new places, something different. Her whole life is lived among the identical houses of her family and friends with just brief respite at the school. Hinted at by her teacher, and just barely imagined, there is another life out there.

'Are you coming back after the summer or helping out at home?' Mrs Murdoch, an austere widow who rarely wasted words, had asked on the last day of school.

'I've tae help,' said Chrissie. Mrs Murdoch nodded and marked up the register. Chrissie didn't expect an argument. Times were hard, everyone knew it.

*

With the baskets safely stowed in the guard's van, Chrissie rushes down the train to find a space in a third-class compartment. Desperate for a window seat, she will fight anyone for the privilege. There are lots of familiar faces. Half the train is folk from Methil and Leven, all wanting to win the pool for first bird home. There is prize-money and club medals too, and all the side bets.

'Lass,' the muttered acknowledgement comes from Jim Fleming, one of their close neighbours, a grey-faced man with sunken eyes and a glutinous, hacking cough which could equally have come from mining or pigeon-keeping. Chrissie is happy to see someone from her street and sits down opposite him, by the coveted window.

'I aye sit facing the engine,' observes Jim, seemingly not wishing to open a conversation as he then stares straight out at the view, puffing fiercely on a thin cigarette, without further regard to Chrissie. She doesn't care. She sits well back, feeling the scratch of the upholstered seat against the backs of her bare legs. She is just as happy to watch familiar sights recede into the distance as to see new ones coming. There are three other men and two women in the compartment by the time the train pulls out with a whistle and gush of steam, and they chatter comfortably amongst themselves.

*

After Ladybank, the haar starts to lift and Chrissie stares at the views out over the countryside. She can see so far into the distance. They live near the seaside in Methil but she hardly ever has time to go to the shore, and never leaves the town. The fields are pale green with growing barley, and cows and sheep graze on the rolling slopes. She has a brief, beguiling vision of life as a farmer. Doubtless hard work, but in the open and unconstrained by the pits, the bings, the rows and rows of crowded cottages. Imagine living here in the fresh air, surrounded by animals and birds of all kinds, not just the doos.

Dragging her gaze away from the window, Chrissie goes to find the toilet and makes her way up the corridor, squeezing past clumps of men who are gossiping and exchanging information about breeding and training methods. Most of the compartment doors are open to relieve the stuffiness of the warm day and folk wander in and out in ones and twos, changing places in a complex social dance. She catches snatches of conversation:

'I telt her no tae gang wi him.'

'He said he'd dae it the morn's morn but I hae ma doots.'

'Ye've tae watch them a' the time at that age.'

'So he's been feeding it up these fower weeks an' hasnae thoct fir a meenit whit's really in the corn.'

Chrissie stops at this and stands just out of sight of the man who has spoken from within one of the compartments. She's recognised his ferrety face. He was talking to Billy in the yard one day when her da was out. She saw him looking out the back gate before slipping into the lane.

'He'll no be sae shair o' hissel noo when that bird cannae flee a hunner yairds.'

'Wheest you. Ye dinnae ken wha micht be listening,' another voice interrupts and the chatter goes down in volume so that Chrissie can't make out any more. She wonders if she could have heard right. Could Billy have been duped into doping his own bird? She feels sick. If Anster Lass doesn't win today, how much will Da and Billy lose? She knows the rent is due and the kitchen press nearly empty. They can't afford to lose this race and they'll likely blame her for some imagined mishandling of the release.

*

At Dunkeld the handlers gather just outside the station where the club official stands ready with the whistle to start the race. All the birds will be released together. Chrissie arranges her baskets so that she can easily pull the straps open and she whispers to the four doos, reassuring them that they will soon be out. The station clock is at twelve and the official raises the whistle to his lips. Then the birds are released and in the hot flurry of wings she tries to keep her eyes on all four to see if they are starting to settle. She sees them circling among the others, establishing their location. Never tempted to stay where they are released, they begin the race back to their own yards.

When the end comes it is so swift and sudden that she almost doesn't see it. The sparrowhawk, a blur of striped wings, speeds from the trees with a singularity of purpose and, as it reaches Anster Lass, it pushes its legs forward, claws outstretched. The doo hasn't a chance. The claws dig hard into the back of her neck and the two birds plummet together, tumbling and spinning towards the ground before the raptor re-establishes control and circles with its helpless prey back under the trees it has come from. Chrissie stands open-mouthed, the gorge rising in her throat as she takes in the magnitude of the disaster.

*

The journey home passes in a haze, with kindly pats on her shoulder which she barely feels. She is in shock, shivering despite the warmth, unable to speak to the people who offer her crumbs of comfort:

'Naebody's fault, lass.'

'It would hae been quick, she wouldnae hae kent whit hit her.'

'Still got ither birds in the race, mind.'

The image of Anster Lass spinning through the air will not leave her. She feels that she saw mute terror in the bird's eyes but she couldn't have, she was too far away. How will she be able to explain what happened? Her fears about the feed will now seem like a stupid lie, invented to cover her own shortcomings.

It is after seven when she pushes open the back gate and finds Da and Billy at the doocot.

'Here she comes,' says Da with a broad grin. 'Weel done, lass, we've got a champion here.'

'What? But Anster Lass ...'

'Aye,' says Billy, 'I d'ae ken whaur she's got tae but Black Jocky came in first and scooped the pool.'

'She was ta'en by a sparrowhawk,' says Chrissie, tears starting to flow.

'Aw, that's a shame, lass, but dinnae greet, it's no your fault.'

'But whit aboot the bets? Huv ye no lost a' yer money?'

Billy winks. 'Ye'll still get yer tanner. I wis getting a wee bit suspicious about the special feed I wis offered, thocht someone wis trying to nobble her. I played it canny and got a pal tae bet against her fir me.'

'Ye kent?' Chrissie stares at Billy, the tears drying on her flushed cheeks.

'Dinnae fash yersel, lass,' says Da. 'Wi' Jocky winning the pool we're a' happy.'

With that, they leave the yard and head for the pub. Chrissie watches the gate slam behind them. She is relieved that they aren't angry, that they haven't lost the money. She stands quite still for several minutes then reaches into the doocot and picks up a water dish. The birds will likely need a drink.

Kate Tough

THE MISSUS

She did not kill herself
enough. Left herself behind
in jackets that hang
and mugs that do not move
between leaving for work
and arriving back.

Here in the tongue
he no longer has to bite
or use at all
very much
alive in his night
she did not kill
herself. She went
killing so much else.

Lynnda Wardle

THE ORDER OF THINGS

My mother has beautiful dresses she wears when it is hot. This morning she chooses the one with blue flowers snaking together, each flower edged in black, the outline trailing away at the stem as though the ink has run out. They are the wildest flowers I have ever seen; nobody's mother wears a dress like this one. The waist is tight; the bodice cuts straight across her freckled chest before the thin straps disappear over her shoulders. I am proud to walk next to this dress, holding the hand at the end of her long brown arm. There are other dresses of course, but this is the one that I want to be near. I love the stiffness of the fabric, the colours and the smell of perfume soaked into the material. It hangs in her cupboard with all the other dresses, some ordinary and some, like this one, are special; a dress to light up the world. We sway down Sixth Street towards the Wishing Well, the beautiful blue sundress trailing a small girl trotting to keep up.

Miss Botha is in charge of the Wishing Well and she has to fold herself in half to reach down to my level. She uses our names at the end of every sentence and says, her voice sing-songing: *How are we this morning, Janet/Tommy/Hannes?* Her breath smells of mint and something rotten. She likes me and gives me chores to do. I have a badge saying *Monitor* which I pin to my shirt every morning. I know how to carry the scissors safely so as not to fall on them or poke someone's eyes out and how to store the glue pots in neat rows, the yellow applicators standing to attention. We have facecloths with our names stitched in curly letters. The cloths hang above the washbasins where we wash our hands before lunch. The toilets are smaller than the one we have at home and there are pictures painted on the doors: Red Riding Hood, three little pigs, the old woman who lived in a shoe, and in the afternoon all the children have a nap in a big room. I never stay after lunch because my mother fetches me and we walk down the road back to our house. We eat peanut butter sandwiches at the kitchen table and then my mother tells me to go and play.

Since I have been attending the Wishing Well, there is an order to my days that I love and makes me feel safe. Mondays are full of promise.

My father wakes me early and prepares breakfast. I sit at the kitchen table, swinging my legs, waiting for a bowl of mielie pap with butter and milk. We listen to the news on Springbok Radio, my father muttering every now and again at a story. Bloody afs, always causing trouble, he'll say, banging his spoon on the side of the porridge pot. I don't know any black people other than Elias who works in the garden on Fridays, but he seems okay and lets me follow him around, dragging his rake from one part of the garden to the next without complaining that I am in his way. My father says that Elias is a good boy, not a troublemaker.

After breakfast, my father leaves for work, carrying his boxy brown briefcase, leaving the smell of Old Spice and cigarette smoke lingering in the air long after he has gone. I get dressed in the clothes my mother puts out for me on the bed, brush my teeth and hair. I have a small suitcase containing an apple or a banana, a spare jersey and Cindy the doll with the odd eyes that open when I hold her upside down. These are my morning routines and I peg my world to them. I travel into the week, head held high, dressed in tartan trousers and a blue knitted jumper, the small suitcase in one hand, the other held tightly by my mother. I am hopeful, trusting in the order of things to keep me safe, from what I am never quite sure, but I know from fairy tales and the sound of branches scratching at my windows at night that there are things to be afraid of, even if I do not yet know their names.

It is called the Wishing Well because there is a fish pond in the front garden and next to it, a stone well with a rope and wooden bucket. The back garden where we play during break has coloured slides, swings with rubber seats made of old tyres and small painted benches, but the front garden with the fish pond is where we would really like to play. We are not allowed in the front garden. It is shaded and full of dark spaces to explore, and although we don't say it to each other, I know that there isn't one child sitting on the safe back-garden benches who doesn't wish they were exploring in the front. The well is shaded by a large tree that blocks out the sun for most of the day. It is a lovely special thing, this wishing well, and when I walk past it on the way into nursery school I strain to see what is in the pond. Occasionally I have seen a flash of gold under the water. We have been told that it is a wishing well because that is what people do when they walk past

– they throw in coins, just small coins like one cent or two cents or maybe five cents if they want a big wish granted. What would I wish for if I had a coin to throw? I think of the box of paper dolls on sale at the chemist for three rand, a fortune and much too expensive to plead for. Or a brother or sister, maybe they are not that expensive. But this is impossible anyway because we are not allowed anywhere near the well and certainly not allowed to throw coins, or even to see into its dark interior where we might catch the copper glint of forgotten wishes under the black water.

One winter morning, Freddy van Zyl does it. He slips away from the group at first break and sneaks around the side of the house, past the metal dustbins and neatly stacked flowerpots and the old petrol cans planted with daisies. Perhaps he circles the well and then somehow loses his footing, stumbling, grabbing the rough stone of the well, or perhaps, made bold by this surge of curiosity, he climbs on to the stone ledge at its base, leaning over to see if there are any fish. I know, we all know, that there are no fish inside the well, how would they eat and it would be too dark surely. But I also know that Freddy is not much of a thinker and perhaps he wasn't really thinking things through at this point in his adventure. We know that the well doesn't have anything for us; that the well is out of bounds, there is nothing there to see children, and it is very very dangerous. For Freddy, perhaps these warnings are like a personal invitation to investigate. Perhaps he picks up a smooth white pebble from the rockery in the sunny part of the garden and carries it, warm as an egg in his hand, to throw into the well. He must count the seconds before he hears the deep *plop* and echo as it hits the water below. Or maybe Freddy just wanted to see how deep the well was and leaned over, surprised to see in the water the reflection of a small face, just like his own, a familiar scrappy cowslick and freckles.

Miss Botha is crying. She makes hiccupping noises when the ambulance comes to fetch Freddy who is pale and streaked with slime. What a stupid *stupid* boy. We line up and wait for our parents to fetch us, all the routines of the day broken up by Freddy and his thoughtlessness. No mid-morning snack or songs in the big room with the out-of-tune piano. I think of Freddy's face, the stupid cowslick and the freckles, how his nose always has a plug of old snot in one nostril and how it flaps in and out when he breathes. The colour of the snot is a greenish yellow and even though Miss Botha wipes it away there is always another to take its place. A disgusting stupid boy, this is the only conclusion I can come to after this well incident, even though we have played together often and he has on occasion made me laugh by pulling his special face involving the squinting of eyes, his tongue lolling sideways out of his mouth. This stupid boy has somehow won the competition; he is the boy at the end of the race taking the tartan ribbon and a big glittery 1. Freddy has won first prize. He has looked into the forbidden place, the place that I wanted to see, but I know that I am a good girl and I listen to Miss Botha. It would no more occur to me to disobey her than to take a crayon and scribble on the walls of the playroom. What he has seen, I can only guess at. Maybe green sludge, or black glittery water rippling in the breeze, but what beyond that? What did he see below the shiny skin of the water? Whatever he saw, it was enough to coax him over, to release his grip and fall over the edge, swallowed by the dark mouth of the well.

What is the punishment likely to be for this act, I wonder? Miss Botha doesn't smack us but usually puts the offender in another room on a special wooden chair for naughty children. I have never been on that chair. I keep my nose clean, as my mother says, I stay out of trouble. Be a good girl and Listen and Do as You're Told are my instructions, and I follow them to the letter. If she is exasperated, Miss Botha shouts a little, her eyes bulging. But she is not shouting at Freddy today, she is just making odd noises and choking into a wad of tissues as the ambulance men strap Freddy onto a stretcher and we stand watching, a forlorn straggle of frightened children. We watch as the men bang the ambulance doors closed, drive off, blue lights flashing although they haven't put the siren on. Why don't they turn on the siren, I wonder, and I am going to ask Miss Botha, but she is waving at us to go inside and she doesn't even get us to line up first. Go inside, all of you, she shouts. Hurry up! Maak gou!

That day my mother fetches me early and we walk home holding hands even though I don't want to. Her grip is too tight and I pull away to balance on the edge of the kerb, wobbling with aeroplane arms, until she tells me to get back on to the pavement. When we get home, she makes spaghetti from a tin. I watch her, wondering why we are having this instead of peanut butter sandwiches. Here you are, she says, fussing a little, straightening the spoon next to the bowl. On Wishing Well days I have a glass of cold milk but today she makes me a hot chocolate which I am usually only allowed on Sundays. She doesn't mention Freddy. I suck strands of spaghetti, letting the ends smack against my lips in a satisfying spatter of tomato sauce, and wonder if I can bring up the subject. Stop that, she says and gets up to fetch me a piece of kitchen roll. The moment seems to have passed and I say nothing. I finish my lunch and wander into the garden to find Elias. He is squatting, digging in the shade. I pick up his rake and pull it behind me, figuring he won't chase me away if I bring a gift. Elias gives me a small garden fork and tells me to loosen the soil in the rose bed. I turn my back to the sun and start digging.

At the Wishing Well, Freddy's adventure leaves us strange with each other for a few days. My best friend Ronnie stops talking to me and sits on her own on a bench in the back garden, picking the scabs on her knees. I don't know what to say to her, so I wander off and spend break time swinging, back and forth, scuffing the toes of my shoes in the sand with each pass, satisfied at the puff of dust I make at every swoop. The grown-ups don't say anything about Freddy and this makes the whole incident even more mysterious. The fact is that he simply isn't there in the mornings, he has *disappeared*. His blue washcloth with *Freddy* in curly letters is still hooked above the washbasin but his place at the snack table has been filled by moving everyone up a seat, and now there is no Freddy space. This gives me an empty feeling as though I am hungry. My mother picks me up every day as usual from the Wishing Well, her smile bright as she greets Miss Botha. I track her face, looking for clues to the disappearance of Freddy, but nothing seems out of the ordinary. Her mouth moves, the red lipstick leaking slightly into the small lines around her mouth. Thank you please yes tomorrow of course. They talk above my head in long sentences that weave in and out with ands and ums and no breathing spaces for me to find a way in. I dig a hole in my tights with a small stick while I wait for them to finish.

When she is done, we walk down the driveway past the wishing well, which now has a thick piece of blue plastic fastened over the opening.

I try not to look at the well. The plastic is out of place and ugly, and the front garden looks bare as though a light has been turned on and all the corners are illuminated. It doesn't look appealing any more, and I walk as quickly as I can through the front gate and past the sign with the bright letters saying *Wishing Well: Fun, Play and Learning Together!* And in smaller letters: *Miss R. Botha, Principal* and a phone number. Underneath the lettering is a drawing of a wishing well with a smiley face on its stone belly, a cheerful red bucket shaded by a lopsided roof.

Roderick Watson

THE SILVER OF OLD MIRRORS

The silver of old mirrors   (slightly foxed)
with float glass made on a molten pool of tin
holds us   (tightly locked)   in its cool embrace.

Touch your finger to the surface   and reach.
It will always be half an inch away from such
likeness   and always other to the one you are.

This as close as we get   brightly boxed in the moment.
The mahogany frame. The finger. Your face. So much
old furniture to keep   to remember   to lose.

So this is what I'm thinking   in the freezing gloom
of a storehouse in Auchterarder   as we wander past
dressing tables and sepulchral wardrobes with their faint air

of mothballs and missing clothes. I see anew
the lines around your eyes   (faintly laced)   and
my own pale face   and want to reach and touch

you again   the thin silk of your skin   to recall
its silver ghost that time in Savannah.
The darkened room. The molten pool of tin.

Jim C. Wilson

GIFTS

There were worlds in cereal packets.

Mastodons and dinosaurs rumbled forth
from cartons of honey-sweet Sugar Puffs.
With paint I gave them life to lumber
across the plains of my tablecloth landscape:
Genesis amongst the plates and milk jug.
I searched the Deep with Shreddies frogmen
who sank, feet first, through 20,000 leagues,
in lemonade bottles that contained the oceans.
And if I, like a god, unscrewed the stopper,
a wee plastic pal, pressure off, rose
buoyant to the surface and bobbed with relief,
unscathed, with his mission accomplished.
Submarines lurked in cornflake packets;
fingers probed through the crackly gold coral
in search of each hard plastic hull. (This fleet,
somehow, was powered by baking powder.)
I chewed through acres of Shredded Wheat
in order to marshal a miniature airforce.
I flew the lot – IN SIX SUPERB COLOURS!

Last year in France I bought some soap powder;
the packet promised *un cadeau*. It was
a soft pink block of scented rubber,
in fact a child's eraser. I left it
lying by the sink, forgot to take it home.

Today I spread some Flora on my toast
aware of a dearth of revelation.

BIOGRAPHIES

Juana Adcock is a writer and translator. Her work has appeared in publications such as *Magma Poetry, Gutter, Glasgow Review of Books, Asymptote* and *Words Without Borders*. Her first book, *Manca*, was considered by distinguished critic Sergio González Rodríguez as one of the best poetry books published in 2014.

Eunice Buchanan was born in Arbroath, where Scots was the lingua franca. When she retired from teaching in 1991, she joined a local writing group and ended up with a PhD in Creative Writing at Glasgow University under the splendid tutelage of Tom Leonard.

Jim Carruth's first chapbook collection was published in 2004. Since then he has brought out a further five chapbooks and an illustrated fable. His poetry has won numerous prizes and in 2014 he was appointed Poet Laureate of Glasgow. His verse novella *Killochries* was published in 2015.

Defne Çizakça is a creative writing PhD candidate at the University of Glasgow where she is writing a historical novel about nineteenth-century Istanbul. She is the fiction editor of *Unsettling Wonder* and the co-editor of three books, *Tip Tap Flat: A View from Glasgow, New Fairy Tales: Essays and Stories* and *Miscellaneous: Writing Inspired by the Hunterian*.

Polly Clark's three collections of poetry, all published by Bloodaxe Books, are *Kiss* (2000), *Take Me With You* (2005) and *Farewell My Lovely* (2009). A new collection, *Lethe*, will appear in 2016. 'Wystan Comes to Helensburgh' is an extract from *Larchfield*, her forthcoming novel based around W. H. Auden's years in Helensburgh.

Terese Coe's poems and translations have appeared in the *TLS, Poetry Review, Agenda, The Threepenny Review, Poetry, New American Writing* and many other publications. Her poem 'More' was heli-dropped across London in the 2012 London Olympics Rain of Poems, and she has a new collection of poems out, *Shot Silk*.

Stewart Conn lives in Edinburgh. His publications include *The Loving-Cup* and *Estuary* (Mariscat Press) and from Bloodaxe, *The Breakfast Room* and most recently a new and selected volume, *The Touch of Time*. His web address is **www.stewartconn.com**; and he can be heard reading from his work on The Poetry Archive.

Gordon Dargie was born in 1951 and brought up in Lanarkshire. He taught English in Lanarkshire and Argyll and from 1980 in Shetland, where he still lives since retiring as Principal of Shetland College. He has two grown-up children. In 2009 Kettillonia published his first collection, *a tunnel of love*.

Anne Donovan is the author of the short story collection *Hieroglyphics and other Stories* (2001) and the novels *Buddha Da* (2003), *Being Emily* (2008) and *Gone Are the Leaves* (2014), all published by Canongate.

Carol Farrelly, awarded a Jerwood/Arvon Mentorship 2015/16, is working on her second novel. She is a previous Robert Louis Stevenson Fellow and Scottish Book Trust New Writer. Her stories have been published in the *Irish Times*, *Stand*, *Edinburgh Review*, *Aesthetica* and *Popshot*, and broadcast on Radio 4. She has been shortlisted for the Bridport, Fish and Asham.

Alec Finlay (1966–), artist, poet and publisher, well known for his use of innovative poetic forms – mesostic, embedded-poem, circle-poem – has published over thirty books; recent publications include *I Hear Her Cry* (2015), *Taigh: a wilding garden* (2014) and a long poem on bees, myth and technology, *Global Oracle* (2014).

Cheryl Follon has published two collections of poetry – both with Bloodaxe Books. She was a finalist in the *Spectator*'s Shiva Naipaul Memorial Prize for essay writing in 2012 and her work has appeared in many places including the *Scotsman*, the *Scottish Review of Books* and on Radio 4.

Lesley Glaister is the prize-winning author of thirteen novels, most recently *Little Egypt*. Her short stories have been anthologised and broadcast on Radio 4. She has written drama for radio and stage. Lesley is a Fellow of the Royal Society of Literature, teaches creative writing at the University of St Andrews and lives in Edinburgh.

Andrew Greig is the author of twenty books of poetry, novels and non-fiction. Born in Bannockburn, raised in Anstruther, he lives in Edinburgh and Orkney, with his wife Lesley Glaister, as a full-time writer and part-time banjoist.

Brian Hamill has lived in Glasgow since 2009. He works as a software developer in the city centre, and serves as Submissions Editor for *thi wurd* magazine. Brian has had stories published in various books and magazines. He was a winner of the Scottish Book Trust New Writers Award, 2013.

Lesley Harrison lives in Angus. Her most recent pamphlet, *Upstream* (2013), grew out of a science/arts collaboration to map the hidden burns and medieval wells beneath Dundee. *Ecstatics: a language of birds* won the 2012 NLS Callum Macdonald Memorial Award.

Sylvia Hays lives in Orkney, which has fed her work as a painter for many years. Now she is far enough away in time and place from her life in America to start writing about it. 'Tissue' is an extract from the memoir she hopes to complete this year.

Jules Jack: raised in Stockbridge, Edinburgh, read lots, spent all holidays with her grandparents in Dundee and Newport-on-Tay. Went to Oxford University. Has two young children and writes from her caravan in Fife. 'In Dundee' is an extract from a novel in progress.

Andy Jackson has several publications to his name including *The Assassination Museum* (2010), *Split Screen* (2012) and *Double Bill* (2014), all Red Squirrel Press, and *Whaleback City: the Poetry of Dundee and its Hinterland* (Dundee University Press, 2013). His new collection, *A Beginner's Guide to Cheating*, is due on Red Squirrel Press in 2015.

Vicki Jarrett is a novelist and short story writer from Edinburgh. Her first novel, *Nothing is Heavy*, was shortlisted for the Saltire Society Scottish First Book of the Year 2013. Her collection of short stories, *The Way Out*, was recently published by Freight Books.

Brian Johnstone's work has appeared throughout Scotland, in the UK, North America and Europe. He has published six collections, most recently *Dry Stone Work* (Arc, 2014), and his work appears on The Poetry Archive website. He has read at festivals from Macedonia to Nicaragua, and venues across the UK.
brianjohnstonepoet.co.uk

Julie Kennedy has published poetry in a number of literary magazines including *Causeway/Cabhsair* and *Southwords*. Mentored by Gerrie Fellows as part of Glasgow Mirrorball's Clydebuilt Mentoring Scheme in 2014. She currently teaches at a secondary school in North Lanarkshire and lives in the south side of Glasgow.

Marcas Mac an Tuairneir is a writer of poetry, prose, drama and journalism, in Gaelic and English. His début collection, *Deò*, was published in 2013, a second, *Lus na Tùise*, and a novel, *Cuairteagan*, are expected this year. In 2014, he won the Highland Literary Salon's prize for poetry and the Baker Prize for Gaelic Writing.

Linda McCann has published poetry and prose. She has been a Hawthorden Fellow, a recipient of a Scottish Arts Council Writer's Award, and has been Writer in Residence for the Universities of Glasgow and Strathclyde. She has honours degrees in English and Law.

Ian McDonough was born and raised in Brora on the east coast of Sutherland, and lives in Edinburgh with his partner and daughter. When not writing he manages the Scottish Community Mediation Centre. His fourth collection, *A Witch Among the Gooseberries*, was published by Mariscat in November 2014.

James McGonigal, Glasgow-based poet and biographer, has most recently co-edited Edwin Morgan's *The Midnight Letterbox: Selected*

Correspondence 1950–2010 (Carcanet Press, 2015). *Living Backwards*, a new collection of poems, is forthcoming from Red Squirrel Press.

Crìsdean MacIlleBhàin/Christopher Whyte is joint editor of the complete poems of Somhairle Mac Gill Eain/Sorley MacLean and has five collections of Gaelic poems to his credit, most recently *An Daolag Shìonach/The Chinese Beetle* (Glasgow University Celtic Department, 2013). A second volume of translations from the Russian of Marina Tsvetaeva, *Milestones*, will appear in 2015.

David Shaw Mackenzie comes from Easter Ross. He now lives in London. He is the author of two novels – *The Truth of Stone* and *The Interpretations* (Sandstone Press, 2013). See more of his work at **davidshawmackenzie.com**.

Kirsten MacQuarrie lives in Glasgow. She is an MLitt student in History of Art at the University of Glasgow. Her poem 'The Clyde' won the 2014 Glasgow Women's Library Mixing the Colours competition, and was published in the *Mixing the Colours* anthology in March 2015.

Ian Madden's short fiction has appeared in the *Edinburgh Review*, *The London Magazine*, *Stand*, *Wasafiri* and has been broadcast on BBC Radio 4.

Susan Mansfield is a writer and journalist who has written about literature and the arts for Scottish newspapers for nearly twenty years. She has written poetry for longer than she cares to remember and her first play, *On the Edge*, was performed in Edinburgh in spring 2015.

Duncan Stewart Muir grew up on an old farm in the Hebrides but has spent most of his adult life in Glasgow, where he teaches English. His poetry has been published in *Gutter*, *The Flight of the Turtle: New Writing Scotland 29*, *Poetry Review*, *PN Review* and *In Protest: 150 Poems for Human Rights*.

Ingrid Murray holds a Masters degree in Creative Writing from the University of Edinburgh. A recent poetry collaboration with the

Edinburgh Makar, Christine De Luca, *A Month on the Mile*, can be listened to on the Scottish Poetry Library website.

Niall O'Gallagher's first book of poems, *Beatha Ùr*, was published by Clàr in 2013. A second, *Suain nan Trì Latha*, will appear in 2016. He lives in Glasgow.

Louise Peterkin lives and works in Edinburgh, as a Library Assistant for Edinburgh University. After a hiatus, she got back into writing after joining a brilliant writers workshop. Much of her poetry is inspired by film and she enjoys creating characters in her poems, giving them a voice and a story.

Peikko Pitkänen is a writer, editor and literary translator who has translated over forty novels. She grew up in Helsinki, Finland, and now lives in Edinburgh, where she completed Napier University's MA programme in Creative Writing. She is a lover of fairy tales, unpredictable seas and remote windswept islands.

Alison Rae is genetically predisposed to idleness. Much to her continued chagrin, she does not have a novel in progress. Instead, she earns a crust by proofreading the books of proper writers who actually have written things. 'The Curry Mouse' is her first piece of published poetry.

Cynthia Rogerson has written four novels and a collection of short stories. Her work has been translated into seven languages and adapted for a *Woman's Hour* drama series. She won the V. S. Pritchett Prize in 2008, and was shortlisted for Scottish Novel of the Year 2011. She is currently a Royal Literary Fellow in Dundee, and programme director of Moniack Mhor Writers' Centre.

Rose Ruane is a visual artist and writer living and working in Glasgow. She has exhibited her visual art widely at home and abroad. She is currently the recipient of the **OffWestEnd.com** Adopt a Playwright award 2015, and is working on her play *Confessions of a Teenage Poltergeist*.

Stewart Sanderson is a third-year PhD student at Glasgow University, working on translation and modern Scottish poetry. His poems have appeared widely in UK and Irish magazines, notably *The Dark Horse*, *Gutter*, *Irish Pages*, *Magma* and *Poetry Review*. In 2014 he was shortlisted for the inaugural Edwin Morgan Award.

Andrew Sclater is a poet, actor and drystane dyker from Edinburgh. He has edited Darwin's letters, and co-founded the National Botanic Garden of Wales. His poetry has won Scottish Book Trust and New Writing North awards, appeared in *Best Scottish Poems 2014*, and been shortlisted for the Picador Poetry Prize.

Shelley Day Sclater was one of Edinburgh UNESCO City of Literature's emerging writers in 2013. Her short fiction has appeared in print and in online literary magazines, in newspapers and anthologies. Her first collection will be published in 2017. Represented by Jenny Brown Associates.

David Scott comes from Gourock on the Firth of Clyde and lives in Cornwall with his family. He had poems in *New Writing Scotland* 5 and is glad to be back.

Nancy Somerville is an Edinburgh-based Glaswegian who writes mainly poetry but also short stories and has finished the first draft of a novel. Her poetry collection *Waiting for Zebras* was published by Red Squirrel Press (Scotland) in 2008.

Dan Spencer lives in Glasgow with his wife and small daughter. His writing has appeared in *Gutter*, *Flash*, *Fractured West* and the *Scotsman*. He won the National Galleries of Scotland's Creative Writing Competition (prose) in 2013. **danspencerwriter.wordpress.com**

A student on the first year of the Masters in Creative Writing at Edinburgh Napier University, **Alison Summers** has submitted a PhD in Creative Writing at Newcastle University, where she wrote a novel about a character with dementia. She read at Story Shop at the 2014 Edinburgh Book Festival.

David Tallach is a former winner of the WH Smith Young Writers' competition in 1991, judged by Ted Hughes, and has had over twenty short stories published on **www.cazart.co.uk** between 2009 and 2013. He has written a children's novel. He is regularly involved in drama at Eden Court Theatre, Inverness.

Karen Thirkell lives on the east coast of Fife, where she spends far too much time staring at the sea. She is currently engrossed in the world of Greek and Roman mythology and is writing a contemporary YA thriller series (with gods).

Kate Tough held a Scottish Literature residency at Cove Park, 2014, and has received two Creative Scotland Awards (2009 fiction and 2013 poetry). Cargo published Kate's debut novel, *Head for the Edge, Keep Walking*. **www.katetough.com**

Lynnda Wardle grew up in Johannesburg and has lived in Glasgow since 1999. In 2007 she received a Scottish Arts Council new writer's grant and is currently working on a memoir. She has had poems and short fiction published in various magazines, including *thi wurd* and *Gutter*.

Roderick Watson was born and educated in Aberdeen, and as a professor (now retired) at the University of Stirling, he writes and lectures widely on Scottish literature. His own poetry has appeared in many anthologies and two main collections, *True History on the Walls* (1977) and *Into the Blue Wavelengths* (2004).

Jim C. Wilson lives in East Lothian. His prose and poetry have been widely published for over thirty years. His fifth collection of poetry is *Come Close and Listen* (Greenwich Exchange). He has taught his Poetry in Practice classes at Edinburgh University since 1994. More information and a blog are at **www.jimcwilson.com**.

Cover image:
Marc Chagall, 'The Blue Fiddler' (1947)
(detail)
Chagall ® / © ADAGP, Paris and DACS,
London 2015
Photo: akg-images

— New Writing Scotland 33 —

New Writing Scotland is the principal forum for poetry and short fiction in Scotland today. Every year we publish the very best from emerging and established writers, and list many of the leading literary lights of Scotland among our contributors.

Published by the
Association for Scottish Literary Studies
www.asls.org.uk

ASLS

£9.95

ISBN 978-1-906841-24-9

9 781906 841249